W9-CLH-783

As problems confront us, how many times will someone say "that's life"? From Scripture and a lifetime of experience and wisdom, Chaplain Black has written for us an excellent playbook dealing with life's challenges.

John Boozman
US Senator (Arkansas)

I might be considered unique in that I've been a member of the United States Senate for twenty-two years and have known Chaplain Barry Black for thirteen of those years. The application for me from this book, and from years of weekly studies with Chaplain Black, is to pursue humility and avoid self-importance—two qualities not typically found in a US senator. And though the ways in which I've been blessed by this book may not be meaningful to other people, you will find your own Fearless Principles in here that will give you the comfort and direction to lighten up, develop your God-given talents, and live fearlessly in a broken and dangerous world, placing your focus on Jesus.

James M. Inhofe
US Senator (Oklahoma)

Chaplain Barry Black has ministered to the military, to the United States Senate, and to believers and seekers everywhere. In *Nothing to Fear*, he speaks to a troubled and anxious time. He offers Fearless Principles designed not to eliminate the presence of fear in our humble lives, but to give us the perspective and strategies necessary to weaken the power that fear can hold over us. One theme running throughout the book—and it's a challenging one amid the busyness of our days—is the need to simplify our lives. So much fear is created by trying to hold on to and manage what is essentially unimportant and unnecessary. Chaplain Black reminds us of what is truly important—faith and prayer, family, lovingkindness. And he gently chides us—why do we complicate things so much?

Tim Kaine
US Senator (Virginia)

NOTHING
TO FEAR

PRINCIPLES & PRAYERS

*to Help You Thrive
in a Threatening World*

BARRY C. BLACK

TYNDALE
MOMENTUM™

*The nonfiction imprint of
Tyndale House Publishers, Inc.*

Visit Tyndale online at www.tyndale.com.

Visit Tyndale Momentum online at www.tyndalemomentum.com.

TYNDALE, Tyndale Momentum, and Tyndale's quill logo are registered trademarks of Tyndale House Publishers, Inc. The Tyndale Momentum logo is a trademark of Tyndale House Publishers, Inc. Tyndale Momentum is the nonfiction imprint of Tyndale House Publishers, Inc., Carol Stream, Illinois.

Nothing to Fear: Principles and Prayers to Help You Thrive in a Threatening World

Designed by Jennifer Ghionzoli

Unless otherwise indicated, all Scripture quotations are taken from the *Holy Bible,* New Living Translation, copyright © 1996, 2004, 2015 by Tyndale House Foundation. Used by permission of Tyndale House Publishers, Inc., Carol Stream, Illinois 60188. All rights reserved.

Scripture quotations marked CEV are taken from the Contemporary English Version, copyright © 1991, 1992, 1995 by American Bible Society. Used by permission.

Scripture quotations marked ESV are taken from the *The Holy Bible,* English Standard Version® (ESV®), copyright © 2001 by Crossway, a publishing ministry of Good News Publishers. Used by permission. All rights reserved.

Scripture quotations marked KJV are taken from the *Holy Bible,* King James Version.

Scripture quotations marked NIV are taken from the *Holy Bible, New International Version,*® NIV.® Copyright ©1973, 1978, 1984, 2011 by Biblica, Inc.® Used by permission. All rights reserved worldwide.

Scripture quotations marked NKJV are taken from the New King James Version,® copyright © 1982 by Thomas Nelson, Inc. Used by permission. All rights reserved.

For information about special discounts for bulk purchases, please contact Tyndale House Publishers at csresponse@tyndale.com or call 800-323-9400.

Library of Congress Cataloging-in-Publication Data
Names: Black, Barry C., author.
Title: Nothing to fear : principles and prayers to help you thrive in a threatening world / Barry C. Black.
Description: Carol Stream, IL : Tyndale Momentum, an Imprint of Tyndale House Publishers, Inc., [2017] | Includes bibliographical references.
Identifiers: LCCN 2016038060 | ISBN 9781496421081 (hc) | ISBN 9781496418685 (sc)
Subjects: LCSH: Fear—Religious aspects—Christianity. | Spiritual life—Christianity. | Prayers.
Classification: LCC BV4908.5 .B53 2017 | DDC 248.8/6—dc23 LC record available at https://urldefense.proofpoint.com/v2/url?u=https-3A__lccn.loc.gov_2016038060&d=DQIFAg&c=6BNjZ EuL_DAs869UxGis0g&r=ZlF6A1J_SMm9xAyjgyDor34CB-fqQRaraBLNVSdnrVo&m=YGAPYif TJK20lOG0ylOnm0LbJP3D7BnrIFrVAng0mW0&s=-EuM0wPeTgdjFlucVlDHiJWDVPfjifHGoj nZW5szSBI&e=

Printed in the United States of America

23	22	21	20	19	18	17
7	6	5	4	3	2	1

CONTENTS

AUTHOR'S NOTE

EARLY IN WORLD WAR II, in his first speech to the House of
Commons after becoming prime minister, Winston Churchill gave
members of Parliament and the British people a dose of reality: "I
have nothing to offer but blood, toil, tears, and sweat."[1] With similar
realism, Jesus sent his disciples into the world with a warning: "I am
sending you out as sheep in the midst of wolves, so be wise as serpents
and innocent as doves."[2]

Have you ever felt as if you're living in a very dangerous world—
like a sheep among wolves? As you log on or tune in to the seemingly
endless news cycles, does it seem as if the world is more threatening
today than ever before, particularly for people of faith? When we hear
about a racially motivated shooting at a church in South Carolina,
the rise of Islamic State across the Middle East, the beheading of
Egyptian Christians, the attacks on Christians in New Delhi, the
aggressive proselytizing effort of the new atheism, or the drifting of
nations from their spiritual moorings, it's easy to feel as if things are
spiraling out of control. We also see how distorted theology has been
used to justify wars, racial inequality, and premeditated pathology,
enslaving people instead of liberating them. People of faith worldwide seem to be experiencing unprecedented levels of discrimination
and oppression.

Believers in God shouldn't be surprised by the realities of a sometimes predatory world. After all, didn't Jesus say that "here on earth you will have many trials and sorrows"?[3]

But didn't he also say, "Take heart, because I have overcome the world"?[4] The apostle Paul warned his protégé Timothy that godly living invites persecution.[5] Are you prepared to live fearlessly in a threatening world?

This book is intended to help you stay fearless by following seven principles that Jesus gave his disciples before sending them into a dangerous world:

- Prepare to be sent (Matthew 10:1; Luke 10:1).
- Do a reality check (Matthew 9:37-38; Luke 10:2-3).
- Thrive in a predatory world (Matthew 10:16-20; Luke 10:3).
- Be as wise as a serpent (Matthew 10:16).
- Be as innocent as a dove (Matthew 10:16).
- Concentrate on the task (Matthew 10:5-8).
- Persevere through rejection (Matthew 10:11-14, 21-23; Luke 10:8-12).

These principles are as relevant in today's world as they were when first written nearly two thousand years ago. They have provided generations with the courage needed to walk fearlessly in dangerous surroundings. They have helped many to avoid the common pitfalls of life and become more productive. They have strengthened marriages and friendships, provided wisdom for parents, and supplied the power to break addictions. They have salvaged the lives of people who were living on the edge, providing a lamp to guide their feet and a light to illumine their path.[6]

As you learn and practice these precepts, you will develop the ability to remain fearless amid the storms of life, survive adversity, and even thrive in a threatening world.

Perhaps you're wondering why our Good Shepherd would send his lambs out among wolves? Perhaps it's because our Shepherd knows that hardship builds strength and character: "We can rejoice, too, when we run into problems and trials, for we know that they help us develop endurance. And endurance develops strength of character, and character strengthens our confident hope of salvation."[7] Perhaps it's because he knows he will protect his sheep, just as David delivered his flock from a lion and a bear.[8] Perhaps our shepherd puts us in a precarious situation because he is always there with us: "Even when I walk through the darkest valley, I will not be afraid, for you are close beside me."[9] Or maybe we are placed in a predatory world because the master provides us with the equipment we need to survive, and he wants us to trust him. When Jesus sent out his disciples, he gave them power to heal the sick, cast out demons, and proclaim the Good News to the people they encountered.[10] Though we don't have all the answers, we know that the one who sends us out is too wise to make a mistake. We can, therefore, face our threatening world without fear.

PREPARE
TO BE SENT

✦

I

PREPARE FOR SOME PARADOXES

WHEN JESUS WAS PREPARING to send his disciples out to practice their ministry, he told them, "Behold, I am sending you out as sheep in the midst of wolves, so be wise as serpents and innocent as doves."[1] This seems to present an impossible situation. How can sheep survive among wolves? How can a serpent and a dove symbolize the same character? In short, how can we reconcile the paradoxes we encounter in life?

Perhaps it would be wise to first seek to understand what Jesus meant by "wise as serpents and innocent as doves." The innocence of the dove refers to gentleness and purity; the wisdom of the serpent has to do with being aware of the presence of evil. A serpent seems to know its enemies and navigates in a way to avoid them. Still, how do we reconcile the differing characteristics of serpents and doves? The Bible teaches us some important principles that can prepare us to live with certain paradoxes and to walk fearlessly in a threatening world.

FEARLESS PRINCIPLE:
Know that God has already given us the gift of salvation

Knowing that God has intervened in our human predicament by giving us the gift of salvation provides a wonderful context for understanding the challenges of living like snakes and doves in a dangerous world. The apostle Paul describes God's gift in these words: "God saved you by his grace when you believed. And you can't take credit for this; it is a gift from God. Salvation is not a reward for good things we have done, so none of us can boast about it."[2]

And let us not forget that the gift of salvation was a costly one. In the words of the apostle Peter, "God paid a ransom to save you from the empty life you inherited from your ancestors. And it was not paid with mere gold or silver, which lose their value. It was the precious blood of Christ, the sinless, spotless Lamb of God."[3] This gift is so special that nothing can ever surpass it. God has literally given us heaven's best. As Paul says in Romans, "He who did not spare his own Son, but gave him up for us all—how will he not also, along with him, graciously give us all things?"[4] God is *all in*. "No good thing does he withhold from those whose walk is blameless."[5] That alone should inspire us to be wise as serpents and innocent as doves.

FEARLESS PRINCIPLE:
Don't let the serpent swallow the dove

Throughout our lives we will be challenged to reconcile the opposites of good and evil. In business, we must learn to reconcile integrity with intense competition. We are sometimes challenged to reconcile complete honesty with self-interest. Sometimes being completely honest may cost us a sale or advancement. We must reconcile absolute truthfulness with long-term progress. Jesus once said to his disciples, "There is so much more I want to tell you, but you can't bear it now."[6] In other words, it isn't always the right time for full disclosure.

According to Rushworth Kidder in *How Good People Make Tough Choices*, most ethical dilemmas involve "right versus right" conundrums: truth versus loyalty, justice versus mercy, the individual versus the community, and the long term versus the short term.

Some people are so hampered in their attempts to reconcile gentleness with prudence that they seek to escape their predicament by omitting one factor or the other. Such a person might say, "In my work and secular activities, I'll be rough and ready. But with my family and at church, I'll be a person of unassailable integrity." This may be letting the serpent swallow the dove with a kind of practical agnosticism. If we are to live fearlessly in a threatening world, we must reconcile these opposites and refuse to allow the shrewdness of the serpent to swallow up the gentleness of the dove.

FEARLESS PRINCIPLE: *Strive to be unmixed with evil*

We must never neglect wisdom in our character and our actions. Refuse to divorce religion from life. The apostle Paul seems to address people who are having difficulty reconciling opposites when he refers to those who "have a zeal for God, but not according to knowledge."[7] We must not sacrifice our integrity but always strive to stay unmixed with evil.

Members of the church in Laodicea had difficulty with this concept. In Revelation 3:15-16, God rebukes them for their failure to stay unmixed with evil: "I know all the things you do, that you are neither hot nor cold. I wish you were one or the other! But since you are like lukewarm water, neither hot nor cold, I will spit you out of my mouth!" This is an indictment of those who have yet to reconcile the shrewdness of the serpent with the innocence of the dove.

FEARLESS PRINCIPLE: *Learn to ward off evil*

Our ability to thrive in a threatening world is directly connected to our willingness to ward off evil. Jesus encourages us to "keep watch and pray, so that you will not give in to temptation."[8] That's a strategy that can enable us to walk with integrity, even in a dangerous world.

The apostle Peter also gives us a firm warning: "Stay alert! Watch out for your great enemy, the devil. He prowls around like a roaring lion, looking for someone to devour. Stand firm against him, and be strong in your faith. Remember that your family of believers all over the world is going through the same kind of suffering you are."[9] That is certainly encouragement to learn how to ward off evil.

James gives us a similar challenge and encouragement: "Humble yourselves before God. Resist the devil, and he will flee from you. Come close to God, and God will come close to you. Wash your hands, you sinners; purify your hearts, for your loyalty is divided between God and the world. Let there be tears for what you have done. Let there be sorrow and deep grief. Let there be sadness instead of laughter, and gloom instead of joy. Humble yourselves before the Lord, and he will lift you up in honor."[10]

The God who commands us to flee from evil stands ready to empower us to reconcile the paradox of the serpent and the dove, as we observe the following guidelines:

- Know that God has already given you the gift of salvation.
- Don't let the serpent swallow the dove.
- Strive to be unmixed with evil.
- Learn to ward off evil.

Once we have reconciled the opposite characteristics of the serpent and the dove, we will be poised to receive and enjoy God's surprises. "Through his mighty power at work within us," he desires to "accomplish infinitely more than we might ask or think."[11]

PURPOSEFUL PRAYER

O Lord our God, giver of everlasting life, nothing can separate us from your limitless love. Empower us to reconcile life's opposites, making us wise as serpents and innocent as doves. Help us to remember that nothing is impossible to those who place their trust in you. May our faith create in us both the desire and the power to do your will. We praise your mighty name. Amen.

2

PREPARE FOR SOME SURPRISES

LATE IN LIFE, C. S. LEWIS wrote a book called *Surprised by Joy*, in which he chronicled his journey from atheism to theism to Christianity and revealed how he learned to enjoy the unexpected ways that God surprises people with his presence and power. Those who would stay fearless in a predatory world must learn to enjoy God's surprises.

My own life has been a journey through which God has surprised me with unexpected transcendent moments. One of my first encounters with him occurred when I saw the starry heavens in a dark, rural sky. To a city boy like me, the stars seemed so splendid and bright that they looked like a fireworks display. I whispered in the night, "What a wonderful world!"

Later, the opportunity to live in the mountains of Peru brought similar emotions of unexpected discovery. Even later, I had a wonderful encounter with the Holy Spirit, who transformed my life and led me into an experiential relationship with Jesus Christ that I could not have anticipated. I have learned to enjoy God's surprises. In the words of the Frankie Laine standard, "Every time I hear a newborn baby cry or touch a leaf or see the sky, then I know why I believe."[1] God has a thousand ways to surprise us by joy. He wants to do in our lives immeasurably, abundantly more than we can ask or imagine.[2] He also promises not to withhold any good thing from us if we do what is right.[3] How then can we learn to enjoy God's surprises?

FEARLESS PRINCIPLE: *Expect the unexpected*

We should expect the unexpected because life has so many twists and turns, and tomorrow isn't promised to us. Given that life can be so unpredictable, James advises us to remember the Lord in all things: "Now listen, you who say, 'Today or tomorrow we will go to this or that city, spend a year there, carry on business and make money.' Why, you do not even know what will happen tomorrow. What is your life? You are a mist that appears for a little while and then vanishes. Instead, you ought to say, 'If it is the Lord's will, we will live and do this or that.'"[4]

We should expect the unexpected because God can do the impossible. Jesus declares, "If you had faith even as small as a mustard seed, you could say to this mountain, 'Move from here to there,' and it would move. Nothing would be impossible."[5] Think of the miracles recorded in Scripture that occurred because people believed God could do the impossible. Patriarchs, prophets, and saints opened up highways through turbulent seas, quenched the heat of fiery furnaces, shut the mouths of lions, and performed countless other amazing deeds by trusting in God's supernatural, miraculous power.

We should expect the unexpected because God desires to keep us from want. Most of us expect God to supply our needs, but what about our wants?[6] He wants to give us a future and a hope and lead us to a desired destination, doing for us more than we can imagine.[7] No wonder the psalmist observes, "The Lord is my shepherd; I have all that I need."[8] Our loving heavenly Father wants to surprise us with good things. He promises to "open the windows of heaven . . . [and] pour out a blessing so great you won't have enough room to take it in!"[9]

We should expect the unexpected because God promises to provide us with a way of escape from temptation.[10] What a surprise that can be! Whenever we're tempted, we must slow things down and look for God's escape hatch, keeping in mind that "only those who are spiritual can understand what the Spirit means."[11] How exciting to know that God desires to keep us from falling and provides us with unexpected solutions to our challenges. When God stopped Abraham from sacrificing Isaac, he provided Abraham with a substitute—"a ram caught by its horns in a thicket"—thereby opening a way of escape from the test.[12]

We should expect the unexpected because even though Jesus promised he will come again, his return will be sudden and unexpected—"like a thief in the night."[13] Matthew's Gospel puts it this way: "As lightning that comes from the east is visible even in the west, so will be the coming of the Son of Man."[14] Jesus has gone to prepare a place for those who love him so that we will be where he is. We should be prepared for that unexpected day.

We should expect the unexpected because God loves a good time, as he demonstrated through the first recorded miracle performed by Jesus: "On the third day a wedding took place in Cana in Galilee. Jesus' mother was there, and Jesus and his disciples had also been invited to the wedding."[15] Jesus and his disciples went to a party that lasted several days, and the wine flowed freely. This is the last place that some conservative Christians would expect to find Jesus, but we should remember that God is the provider of every good thing, and he enjoys a good time. Anyone who has visited an aquarium and seen the beautiful, colorful, and often bizarre aquatic life that is normally hidden from our view can testify to God's sense of fun and his love of bold and bountiful beauty.

Have you learned to appreciate the importance of joyful living? Are you strengthened and sustained by God's joy?[16] Are you like David, who danced before the Lord?[17] How much dancing goes on in your worship? Joyful living involves singing, dancing, and celebrating; it involves enjoying the feast. Please don't forget that God enjoys a good time.

We should expect the unexpected because Jesus wants us to fully experience life: "The thief comes only to steal and kill and destroy; I have come that they may have life, and have it to the full."[18] God isn't trying to rain on your parade; he wants you to experience the great pleasure of fellowship with him. He wants you to drink fully from the well of abundant life. As Jesus said to the woman at the well in Samaria, "Everyone who drinks this water will be thirsty again, but whoever drinks the water I give them will never thirst. Indeed, the water I give them will become in them a spring of water welling up to eternal life."[19] Jesus can lead us to thirst-free living, even in a dangerous world.

In John 5, Jesus encounters a man who has been lying beside the pool of Bethesda for thirty-eight years, waiting for someone to help him into the water at the opportune moment to receive healing. Jesus asks this man what seems like a strange question: "Do you want to get well?"[20] Wellness and wholeness are what he desires for each of us.

When the disabled man responds affirmatively to Jesus' question, he's met with a challenge from the Lord: "Stand up, pick up your mat, and walk!"[21] In other words, "Do the impossible!"

When the man obeyed and made the effort, he was made whole—physically, mentally, emotionally, socially, and spiritually.[22]

FEARLESS PRINCIPLE: *Give Jesus your challenges*

At the Cana wedding feast, the host ran out of wine, which could have been a real embarrassment. How often do we face similar problems in our day-to-day lives? No matter how blessed we may be, we will eventually be faced with some form of challenge—or even adversity. As with the homes built on rock or sand in Jesus' parable in Matthew 7:24-27, the storms come regardless of the foundation of our lives. The storms hit the just and unjust, the righteous and unrighteous. In living out our days, our joy will eventually be threatened by a change of circumstances.

But that doesn't leave us bereft. Regardless of life's challenges, we can remain fearless by taking our problems to Jesus. When his mother, Mary, said to him, "They have no more wine," it seems she was obeying the wise admonition later recorded by Peter: "Give all your worries and cares to God, for he cares about you."[23]

Jesus says in Matthew 11:28, "Come to me, all of you who are weary and carry heavy burdens, and I will give you rest." He stands ready to help us with our struggles and to strengthen us to meet our challenges. We simply need to take our challenges to him. As it says in the Psalms: "Call on me when you are in trouble, and I will rescue you."[24] Don't miss this opportunity; don't let it be said that "you do not have because you do not ask God."[25]

FEARLESS PRINCIPLE: *Practice prompt obedience*

When Mary brought this challenge before Jesus, he responded that this moment was not a good time for him to act: "My time has not yet come."[26] It was an unexpected response, but Mary was undaunted. She simply went to the servants and said, "Do whatever he tells you."[27] In other words, she encouraged them to listen to Jesus and practice prompt obedience. She knew that Jesus would find a way to help her meet this challenge, and he did.

Turning to the servants, Jesus said, "Fill the jars with water." After they filled six large water jars, he told them, "Now dip some out and take it to the master of ceremonies."[28]

"Do whatever he tells you" is still good advice today. Practice prompt obedience, and God will help you meet your challenges.

And yes, that means we should obey even when we don't understand, even when we think we've already done everything possible. When Jesus comes to Peter in Luke 5 and says, "Go out where it is deeper, and let down your nets to catch some fish," Peter is surprised by this unexpected request.[29] After all, Jesus was a carpenter and Peter was an experienced fisherman who had fished unsuccessfully all night long.

Even though Peter says to Jesus, "Master, we worked hard all last night and didn't catch a thing," he quickly adds, "But if you say so, I'll let the nets down again."[30] Responding with obedience, he found the unexpected: nets so full of fish that they began to tear![31] When we obey even when we don't fully understand, unexpected blessings inevitably ensue.

FEARLESS PRINCIPLE: *Expect God to save the best for last*

My favorite part of the story about Jesus changing the water into wine is the response of the wine taster, the master of the feast. When the servants brought him what they had drawn from the water jars, he was astonished by the quality: "A host always serves the best wine first," he said. "Then, when everyone has had a lot to drink, he brings out the less expensive wine. But you have kept the best until now!"[32] God delights in doing the unexpected in our lives, saving the best for last.

Everything we do should be to glorify God so that every season of our lives will be exemplary.[33] When Moses, the leader who led the Israelites to the Promised Land, disobeyed God and was told he couldn't enter Canaan with the rest of the people, Moses was disappointed.[34] But God saved the best for last. In the New Testament story of the Mount of Transfiguration, we unexpectedly encounter Moses on the mountain, encouraging Jesus, who was soon on his way to Calvary.[35] Moses is one of only a few people to appear in both the Old and New Testaments. God saved the best for last.

One year for my son's birthday, I wanted to surprise him with a gift that would bring a look of joy to his face. I listened carefully for his hints and ideas and then I made my purchase. Our family was at the restaurant of my son's choosing when, at the end of the evening, I presented the gift, which he received with effusive delight and gratitude. Not only did he get a gift that he desired, but I also received a priceless gift of my own: seeing my son respond to the unexpected gift with great joy.

If a parent can experience such delight at the joy of a child, think how our heavenly Father must respond to our joy and gratitude. He is far more generous, kind, and merciful than any human parent, and he takes delight in surprising us with joy. He wants us to experience life to the fullest, and he has given us principles and commandments to keep us from the pitfalls of sin. He surrounds us with the shield of his favor, and he delights in surprising us in the eleventh hour.

———————————

Enjoy God's surprises, for he has promised not to withhold any good thing if we will walk blamelessly.[36] As you seek to stay fearless in a predatory world, enjoy the abundant living that God desires for you to experience as you give him your challenges and wait eagerly to follow his commands. Forget what lies behind you—that's history. Instead, reach toward the future, knowing that the best is yet to come as you apply these principles to your life:

- Expect the unexpected.
- Give Jesus your challenges.
- Practice prompt obedience.
- Expect God to save the best for last.

PURPOSEFUL PRAYER

Eternal God, thank you for the joy of your surprises. You do more for us than we can ask or imagine. Keep our hearts steadfast toward you. Lead us safely to the refuge of your choosing, for we know you desire to give us a future and a hope. Today, give us the power to do your will as we more fully realize that we are servants of heaven and stewards of your mysteries and your blessings. Give us the wisdom to make our faith the litmus test by which we evaluate each action, as we refuse to deviate from the path of integrity. Keep us from being careless about our spiritual and moral growth. We trust in your mighty name. Amen.

3

PREPARE THE SOIL
OF YOUR HEART

PEOPLE OF FAITH are sent into a predatory world as lambs in the midst of wolves. What qualifies us to be sent? What capabilities does God expect from his ambassadors? He expects us to be prepared for his fruit to be produced in and through us. To that end, he desires that we become the right kind of "soil." We gain some insight about this interesting qualification in Jesus' story of the four soils, found in Matthew 13:1-9:

> Later that same day Jesus left the house and sat beside the lake. A large crowd soon gathered around him, so he got into a boat. Then he sat there and taught as the people stood on the shore. He told many stories in the form of parables, such as this one: "Listen! A farmer went out to plant some seeds. As he scattered them across his field, some seeds fell on a footpath, and the birds came and ate them. Other seeds

fell on shallow soil with underlying rock. The seeds sprouted quickly because the soil was shallow. But the plants soon wilted under the hot sun, and since they didn't have deep roots, they died. Other seeds fell among thorns that grew up and choked out the tender plants. Still other seeds fell on fertile soil, and they produced a crop that was thirty, sixty, and even a hundred times as much as had been planted! Anyone with ears to hear should listen and understand."

This story helps us understand how the condition of our hearts can be compared to the types of soil that our faith grows from. In Matthew 13:19-23, Jesus explains the meaning of the different soils:

> The seed that fell on the footpath represents those who hear the message about the Kingdom and don't understand it. Then the evil one comes and snatches away the seed that was planted in their hearts. The seed on the rocky soil represents those who hear the message and immediately receive it with joy. But since they don't have deep roots, they don't last long. They fall away as soon as they have problems or are persecuted for believing God's word. The seed that fell among the thorns represents those who hear God's word, but all too quickly the message is crowded out by the worries of this life and the lure of wealth, so no fruit is produced. The seed that fell on good soil represents those who truly hear and understand God's word and produce a harvest of thirty, sixty, or even a hundred times as much as had been planted!"

The parable describes four kinds of soil: *footpath, rocky, thorny,* and *good.* Which are you? Are you ready to become the kind that God can use to bring a great harvest? On the footpath, the seeds don't even penetrate the soil. They don't sprout, much less grow, but are carried off by the birds. The rocky soil is a bit better, but the lack of depth to establish roots kills its productivity. In the third kind, the seeds germinate but are choked by the thorns of worry and greed. Only the good soil is deep and rich and produces fruit.

God's desire for us to be fertile, productive soil goes all the way back to the beginning. In fact, his first command to humanity was: "Be fruitful and multiply. Fill the earth and govern it."[1] We were created to be productive in each of life's seasons. Psalm 92:12-14 puts it this way: "The godly will flourish like palm trees and grow strong like the cedars of Lebanon. For they are transplanted to the Lord's own house. They flourish in the courts of our God. Even in old age they will still produce fruit; they will remain vital and green." Wow! God expects us to be productive even during the winter of our lives. In other words, even our retirement years should be a productive season.

Productivity is so important to God that he uses it as a means of testing our fitness to serve. Jesus said, "Just as you can identify a tree by its fruit, you can identify people by their actions."[2] Yes, God's servants are known by what they produce. This fruit comes from our connection to Jesus, for he is the vine and we are the branches.[3] As people of faith, we produce fruit not to receive our salvation, but in response to God's gift of redemption to those who remain connected to him.

As we seek to thrive in a dangerous world, we must focus on sowing seeds of faith and leave the results to God. Although we plant seeds, we don't know which ones will prosper or what type of harvest will come. Ecclesiastes 11:6 encourages us with these words: "Plant your seed in the morning and keep busy all afternoon, for you don't know if profit will come from one activity or another—or maybe both."

We are called to plant seeds and then to trust the Lord of the harvest to bring the increase. As the apostle Paul reminds the Corinthians: "I planted the seed in your hearts, and Apollos watered it, but it was God who made it grow."[4] And Paul speaks again in Galatians 6:9: "Let's not get tired of doing what is good. At just the right time we will reap a harvest of blessing if we don't give up. We plant knowing that perseverance is critical because an interval of growth inevitably exists between seedtime and harvest. We don't plant on Wednesday and reap on Friday. Therefore, we must stay the course and persevere. We must be willing to wait for God. "Wait patiently for the Lord. Be brave and courageous. Yes, wait patiently for the Lord."[5] How then can we prepare to be people whom God can use productively in a dangerous world?

FEARLESS PRINCIPLE: *Live productively*

To become prepared for God to send us into a dangerous harvest field, we must live productively ourselves. Every season of our lives should be characterized by fruitfulness, which will enable us to meet God's expectations: "Do your best to improve your faith. You can do this by adding goodness, understanding, self-control, patience, devotion to God, concern for others, and love. If you keep growing in this way, it will show that what you know about our Lord Jesus Christ has made your lives useful and meaningful."[6]

God commands us to become productive problem solvers.[7] He expects us to subdue the challenges in each of life's seasons. He uses people in all seasons of life—think of Noah, Moses, Elijah, Elisha, Mordecai, Esther, Daniel, Mary, and Simeon, for example. Even those who were advanced in years, such as Moses, Elijah, and Simeon, remained faithful in their service to God's Kingdom. God expects us all to serve his purpose in our generation.[8] When we permit him to strengthen us to serve even in dangerous times, we can expect success. "All glory to God, who is able, through his mighty power at work within us, to accomplish infinitely more than we might ask or think."[9]

FEARLESS PRINCIPLE: *Open your mind to truth*

If we are to become the right kind of soil to bring forth fruit in a threatening world, we must remain open-minded. Some people believe that Scripture has no knowledge to impart that cannot be discovered through science or experience. They see religion as a fanciful flight from reality, a phenomenon so otherworldly that it's of no earthly good. On the other hand, some religious people read the Bible but close their minds to what it says. Perhaps the apostle Paul is referring to both in Galatians 4:16: "Have I now become your enemy because I am telling you the truth?" Some people are so opposed to the truth that they shut their minds and hearts to it. These people are like the soil on the footpath in Matthew 13:4; the birds come and devour the seeds of truth before they can sprout or take root. I have observed that God can use us more fully when we open our minds to seeing and accepting by faith his miraculous workings in the world and in our lives.

FEARLESS PRINCIPLE: *Think things through*

Even if we avoid being like the footpath, our hearts may still be like the rocky soil: "The seeds of truth sprout quickly because the soil is shallow, but the plants soon wilt under the hot sun, and because they don't have deep roots, they die."[10] We must think through our decisions and weigh the rights and wrongs of our actions so we're prepared for the seeds of faith to be planted.

We must ensure that there is sufficient depth to our faith to withstand the withering heat of our challenging times. We don't want our faith and our fruitfulness to be scorched by the difficulties of life and wither away. Perhaps this is one reason why the Bible advises us to be "fully convinced" in our minds.[11]

Thinking things through is a protective measure in a predatory world. We need to consider the costs and benefits of our choices, heeding the wisdom of Jesus: "Suppose one of you wants to build a tower. What is the first thing you will do? Won't you sit down and figure out how much it will cost and if you have enough money to pay for it?"[12]

God gave us sound minds for good reason. He expects us to love him passionately with all our minds[13] and to use our minds as we interact with him: "Come now, let us reason together, says the Lord."[14]

God wants you and me to become persuaded regarding the validity of his truth. How vital it is not to underestimate the importance of thinking things through.

FEARLESS PRINCIPLE:
Don't crowd out the important things

In Jesus' parable, the third type of soil has thorns. This can happen when the seeds of truth are choked out by the cares of this life, the deceitfulness of riches, and a desire for worldly things. Another way to describe this is to say that we're majoring in minors and minoring in majors.

How can we so badly misplace our priorities? We find a good example in the story of Mary and Martha in Luke 10. The sisters live in Bethany and are blessed to receive a visit from Jesus. While Mary sits at Jesus' feet, listening to the truth-filled statements that fall from his lips, Martha prepares a meal in accordance with the cultural expectations at the time. As the visit progresses, she becomes upset because Mary is not helping her with the hospitality chores. When Martha finally approaches Jesus and makes her case, she must have been astounded by his response: "Martha, Martha! You are worried and upset about so many things, but only one thing is necessary. Mary has chosen what is best, and it will not be taken away from her."[15] We must not permit life's seemingly necessary things to crowd out things of eternal value.

FEARLESS PRINCIPLE: *Translate hearing into action*

The right kind of soil in Jesus' parable is described as ground that "produced a crop that was thirty, sixty, and even a hundred times as much as had been planted!"[16] This refers to people who hear and understand God's words—and act on them.[17] This is precisely what James admonishes us to do: "Obey God's message! Don't fool yourselves by just listening to it. If you hear the message and don't obey it, you are like people who stare at themselves in a mirror and forget what they look like as soon as they leave."[18] In short, hearing must translate into action or else it amounts to little.

What are the actions that God desires from us? Jesus describes them in the Gospel of Matthew:

> You are like salt for everyone on earth. But if salt no longer tastes like salt, how can it make food salty? All it is good for is to be thrown out and walked on. You are like light for the whole world. A city built on top of a hill cannot be hidden, and no one would light a lamp and put it under a clay pot. A lamp is placed on a lampstand, where it can give light to everyone in the house. Make your light shine, so that others will see the good that you do and will praise your Father in heaven.[19]

What a beautiful description of productive living and the soil that God can keep fearlessly and productively fruitful, even in a predatory world. God wants us to be salt and light in our dangerous world.

What's the advantage of being salt? In the time of Christ, salt was a precious commodity, and we're precious to God. Salt brought flavor and zest to food, just as people of faith should make the environment more palatable. Does your presence add spice to the lives of others? Also, in Jesus' time, salt was a preservative; it kept meat from spoiling, holding putrefaction at bay. Is our nation and world safer because of your life? Do your intercessory prayers make our world more secure? In Genesis 18:16-33, Abraham intercedes with God to spare Sodom and Gomorrah, and he prevails. God agrees to spare those cities for the sake of ten righteous people. Like salt, those who were righteous would release preservation power. Sadly, not even ten righteous people could be found there, and the cities were brought to destruction.[20]

Moreover, salt creates thirst for something more. Does your life do that? Do you possess such exemplary ethical excellence that people want what you have? In John 4, Jesus encounters a Samaritan woman at a well. He promises to quench her thirst by creating an internal spring so that she would never thirst again. It is her interaction with Jesus, however, that sparks in her a desire for something more. When your heart is cultivated to be the right kind of soil, you'll be able to help others become thirsty for a better life.

We are also called to be light bearers in a dark world.[21] Why? Because light dispels darkness; it illuminates and reveals. We should, therefore, live lives that spread God's divine light. The prophet Isaiah describes the kind of life that is a light to the world:

> Share your food with the hungry,
> and give shelter to the homeless.
> Give clothes to those who need them,
> and do not hide from relatives who need your help.
> Then your salvation will come like the dawn,
> and your wounds will quickly heal.
> Your godliness will lead you forward,
> and the glory of the Lord will protect you from behind.
> Then when you call, the Lord will answer.
> "Yes, I am here," he will quickly reply.
> "Remove the heavy yoke of oppression.
> Stop pointing your finger and spreading vicious rumors!
> Feed the hungry,
> and help those in trouble.
> Then your light will shine out from the darkness,
> and the darkness around you will be as bright as noon.[22]
> ISAIAH 58:7-10

FEARLESS PRINCIPLE: *Spend your life; don't hoard it*

As you seek to become salt and light in a threatening world, strive to *spend* your life instead of hoarding it. God has given each of us at least one talent to use in service to our generation.[23]

Jesus underscores this important principle when he says, "If any of you wants to be my follower, you must give up your own way, take up your cross, and follow me. If you try to hang on to your life, you will lose it. But if you give up your life for my sake, you will save it."[24] What wonderful guidance this is on how to spend your life instead of hoarding it.

Giving up our own way is described in other translations as *denying* ourselves.[25]

But how do we do that?

When Peter denied Jesus after his arrest, he said, "I don't even know that man!"[26] And he denied him three times—he was adamant. When we deny ourselves, we seek to do something similar, though in reverse: Instead of denying God, we distance ourselves from our own selfish demands. We ignore what our *self* wants and instead concern ourselves with what *God* wants, particularly when it comes to temptation and sin.

In Romans, the apostle Paul challenges us to deal with ourselves even more decisively: "You must think of yourselves as *dead* to the power of sin."[27] A corpse isn't tempted, seduced, or challenged. When we confront temptation and respond as if we are dead to it, it will empower us to remain fearless as we surrender our lives for the sake of God's Kingdom.

Spending our lives instead of hoarding them involves focusing on *giving* rather than receiving. This strategy is actually counterintuitive. Jesus said that "it is more blessed to give than to receive."[28] But do we really believe that? Most people seem to live as if the opposite were true: It's better to *get* than to give. But if we're preparing our hearts to be good productive soil, we should not only give willingly, but ask ourselves, "*How much* can I give?"

In striving to answer this question, we must be prepared to go beyond the minimum. Jesus challenges us to do this in the Sermon on the Mount: "If you are kind only to your friends, how are you different from anyone else? Even pagans do that."[29] That's a critical question to ask ourselves: How are we any different? Too often, we're satisfied to settle for the minimum, but becoming the right kind of soil entails striving for the maximum.

When we strive for the maximum, we prepare ourselves for "second-mile living." Jesus said it this way: "If anyone forces you to go one mile, go with them two miles."[30] And then he raises the bar even further: "Love your enemies! Pray for those who persecute you! In that way, you will be acting as true children of your Father in heaven. . . . If you love only those who love you, what reward is there for that?"[31] Second-mile living will motivate us to remain fearless enough to love even our enemies, becoming soil that God can use for his glory even in dangerous times.

Kahlil Gibran, a Maronite-Christian poet who emigrated from Lebanon to the United States at the turn of the twentieth century, provides us with great advice on becoming the right kind of soil when it comes to giving. Echoing the sentiments of Jesus from the Sermon on the Mount, Gibran writes, "You give but little when you give of your possessions. It is when you give of yourself that you truly give. For what are your possessions but things you keep and guard for fear you may need them tomorrow? And tomorrow, what shall tomorrow bring to the over-prudent dog burying bones in the trackless sand as he follows the pilgrims to the holy city? . . . All you have shall someday be given; therefore give now, that the season of giving may be yours and not your inheritors."[32] In other words, spend your life; don't hoard it.

———————

We remain fearless in a dangerous world by allowing God to help us become the right kind of soil: soil that God can use in a wholesome and productive way; soil that will bring forth exponential growth—thirtyfold, sixtyfold, and even one-hundredfold. Simply practice the following principles:

- Live productively.
- Open your mind to truth.
- Think things through.
- Don't crowd out the important things.
- Translate hearing into action.
- Spend your life; don't hoard it.

PURPOSEFUL PRAYER

Heavenly Father, help us today to become the right kind of soil so that our lives will be productive for the glory of your Kingdom. Show us how to do things your way, embracing your precepts and walking on your path. Remind us that the narrow and difficult road leads to life and abundant joy. As you teach us to live abundantly, replace our anxiety with calm, our confusion with clarity, and our despair with hope. May your heavenly peace, which transcends human understanding, guard our hearts and minds today and always. We glorify your great name. Amen.

DO A
REALITY CHECK

———— ✦ ————

4

EMBRACE LOVE

FOR MOST OF MY LIFE, I have been fascinated by the magic of love. I have often felt that, even if I didn't believe in God, my exposure to the power of love would be sufficient to push me toward faith in him. Love's power astounds me. I don't understand how we can meet someone with whom we have no blood ties and suddenly feel as if all the good in the world would be dramatically diminished without that person in our lives. How can it be that when we gaze at a newborn son or daughter or grandchild, we suddenly feel an unconditional positive response and regard? In an instant, we become willing to die for that newly arrived bundle. I have trouble wrapping my mind around the supernatural power of love at work in the world.

Unfortunately, it seems we sometimes trivialize love, using the same word to describe our affection for a parent, child, or spouse as we do for our enthusiasm about a candy bar. This seems to devalue that wonderful word, ignoring its nuanced complexity, its power to vivify, and its capacity to inspire. "It always protects, always trusts, always hopes, always perseveres. Love never fails."[1]

Looking at the original Greek language of the New Testament can help us recover the nuances of love because Greek has at least four words for it. *Eros* describes romantic love, the kind we see in Edgar Allan Poe's poem about the beautiful Annabel Lee, whose presence invited the lyrical inspiration of the muse. Second, we have *phileo*, which describes a reciprocal love, such as when we love those who love us. The third Greek word is *storge*, describing parental love. And perhaps the highest form of love is expressed by the word *agape*, which refers to God's perfect unconditional love operating in the human heart. This love releases a power that creates a redemptive goodwill for humankind. It's an overflowing affection that seeks nothing in return. Those who would stay fearless in a predatory world should strive to attain agape love.

Love's crowning achievement is the sacrificial and voluntary giving of one's life for another. John 15:13 describes it this way: "There is no greater love than to lay down one's life for one's friend." These are Jesus' words, referring not merely to martyrdom, but to sacrificing one's life for the good of others. It means living so that we can give an affirmative response to the five questions we will be asked on Judgment Day: "Lord, when did we ever see you hungry and feed you? Or thirsty and give you something to drink? Or a stranger and show you hospitality? Or naked and give you clothing? When did we ever see you sick or in prison and visit you?"[2]

Perhaps it was such sacrificial giving of our lives that Paul had in mind when he wrote, "Present your bodies as a living sacrifice."[3] Is that not what we do when we reach out to the lost, the last, the least, the marginalized, and the lonely?

God calls us to approach this outreach willingly, not grudgingly or out of necessity. "For God loves a person who gives cheerfully."[4] He made us free, moral agents, not robots, so that we could serve him volitionally and not through coercion. He doesn't want robots; he wants loving human beings with the power to make their own choices. God didn't program us with the instincts of homing pigeons, but instead he enabled us even to go against the will of our heavenly Father.

What then must we do to embrace love's crowning achievement?

FEARLESS PRINCIPLE: *Demonstrate real love*

To embrace love's crowning achievement—the voluntary sacrifice of ourselves for the good of others—we must demonstrate real love. Fortunately, God does not leave us to guess what real love should look like. Paul describes it in his first letter to the church at Corinth: "Love is patient and kind. Love is not jealous or boastful or proud or rude. It does not demand its own way. It is not irritable, and it keeps no record of being wronged."[5] Real love is not an abstract concept; it's an active verb—something we *do*. We show our love through commitment and obedience by being patient, kind, humble, helpful, conciliatory, forgiving, honoring, and preferring others to ourselves. Jesus himself calls us to demonstrate genuine love: "If you love me, obey my commandments."[6]

FEARLESS PRINCIPLE: *Show your true identity*

If you were hauled into court for being a servant of Jesus Christ, would there be enough evidence to convict you? The world will not know our true identity by our theological orthodoxy, but by our love. Jesus said, "Your love for one another will prove to the world that you are my disciples."[7]

How well do we as Christians show our love? We have more than two hundred Protestant denominations, and Sunday morning worship times are still one of the most segregated hours of the week. We sing "In Christ There Is No East or West"[8] or "We are not divided, All one body we,"[9] but are we demonstrating this unity in our living? How often do our churches have pulpit exchanges or guest choirs?

When was the last time you worshiped with a diverse congregation, in which most of the attendees didn't look like you? Only by our love will the world see our true identity as disciples of Jesus Christ.

Real love celebrates diversity. In fact, if we don't like diversity, we probably won't like heaven. The apostle John describes those who will enter heaven with these words: "After this I saw a vast crowd too great to count, from every nation and tribe and people and language, standing in front of the throne and before the Lamb. They were clothed in white robes and held palm branches in their hands. And they were shouting with a great roar, 'Salvation comes from our God who sits on the throne and from the Lamb!'"[10] What an amazing experience to worship with people from every nation, tribe, and language. What an incredible encounter with God's diversity and love.

FEARLESS PRINCIPLE:
Pursue the most excellent way that exceeds all other gifts

Agape love exceeds all other spiritual gifts. We've each been given a gift to use to edify those we serve, but nothing compares to agape love.[11] Paul writes, "Eagerly desire the greater gifts. And yet I will show you the most excellent way. If I speak in tongues of men or of angels, but do not have love, I am only a resounding gong or a clanging cymbal."[12] Paul is saying that love is the crowning gift that exceeds all others. And even if we give all we have to the poor and die as martyrs, our actions are meaningless without love.

FEARLESS PRINCIPLE: *Move to the next higher level*

Before leaving the earth, Jesus said to his disciples, "A new command I give you: Love one another. As I have loved you, so you must love one another."[13]

It's important to note that the love Jesus challenges us to possess can be *commanded*; thus, it is more than an emotion. You can't reasonably command an emotion.

Jesus also tells us to love others as he loved us. This means we must love the unlovable and the unworthy. "Love your enemies, bless those who curse you, do good to those who hate you, and pray for those who spitefully use you and persecute you."[14]

This takes us to the higher level of agape. Those who will stay fearless in a predatory world must embrace agape. This was the love that motivated Martin Luther King Jr. to practice a nonviolent direct action that aroused the conscience of a nation and caused walls of racial discrimination to fall.

Those who reach this higher level will not have to worry about God's commandments, for his entire law is summed up in two interconnected statements: "Love the Lord your God with all your heart, all your soul, and all your mind" and "Love your neighbor as yourself."[15] All divine laws hang on these two principles. Paul affirms these principles in two of his letters: "Love does no wrong to others, so love fulfills the requirements of God's law" and "The whole law can be summed up in this one command: 'Love your neighbor as yourself.'"[16]

Let's prepare to thrive in a predatory world. Instead of concentrating on a few hundred rules and regulations, let's fulfill God's law by loving other people. It's the "CliffsNotes" route to theological excellence, a litmus test for our every action. Simply ask yourself these questions:

- Will this decision empower or hinder my love for God and humankind?
- Will this relationship make me more or less loving?
- Will this vocational choice enable me to fulfill the law of love or compel me to permit the ends to justify the means?

We can fulfill God's love simply by loving others as we love ourselves. So there we have it: Embrace love's crowning achievement and stay fearless in a predatory world by sacrificially and voluntarily giving your life for others. Join Jesus in his messianic mission to uplift the least of these among us, proving the sincerity of our commitment and exceeding any other gift we can bring to God. As we strive to make our love *active* by being patient, kind, humble, and hopeful, we will fulfill the law of Christ, and people will know our true identity. This will happen when we remember that love is an action more than an emotion. As we love others as Jesus did, we will learn to love the unlovable by hating the sin but loving the sinner.

To sum it up, we should embrace love's crowning achievement by doing the following:

- Demonstrate real love.
- Show your true identity.
- Pursue the most excellent way that exceeds all other gifts.
- Move to the next higher level.

PURPOSEFUL PRAYER

God our Shield, we embrace today the crowning achievements of your love. Lord, look with favor upon us today. Enable us to go from strength to strength as we learn to thrive fearlessly in a threatening world. Guide us around the obstacles that hinder us from living for your glory as we seek to fulfill your purpose for our lives in this generation. As we strive to please you, empower us to stand for right and leave the consequences to you. We praise your holy name. Amen.

5

PREPARE TO SERVE

IF GOD WERE SEEKING a person for a special assignment, how would you measure up? Would you even qualify for an interview, or would you lack the minimum requirements? Few things help us stay fearless in a threatening world more than knowing that God desires to use us for his glory. It would bring me a wonderful peace to know that my life pleases my Creator and that he endorses me.

God looks for committed servants to accomplish challenging assignments to advance his Kingdom. He sought and found David, whom he called "a man after my own heart," as King Saul's replacement.[1] In John 4, Jesus tells the woman at the well that God seeks "true worshipers [who] will worship the Father in spirit and in truth."[2] In Job 1, God converses with Satan and asks him, "Have you noticed my servant Job? He is the finest man in all the earth. He is blameless—a man of complete integrity. He fears God and stays away from evil."[3] In Job, God found a man who could endure trials with faith, keeping himself unspotted from a dangerous world.

God selected Rebekah to become Isaac's wife,[4] and he chose Zechariah and Elizabeth to be the parents of John the Baptist.[5] God also picked Mary and Joseph to be the earthly parents of the Messiah.[6]

Imagine being handpicked by God, from among everyone else on earth, to be the parents of his Son. These heroes and heroines of faith—and others—show us character traits that enable us to measure up to God's divine standard. Job and David possessed reverence, integrity, humility, faith, and piety. With Job, Elijah, Daniel, and the wise virgins, we see people who improved their talents, developed their energies, exercised common sense, and displayed godliness. By examining the lives of some who were selected by God for service, we prepare ourselves to better please him so he can use us powerfully for his special purposes in a dangerous world. How should those who want to be fully used by God prepare themselves?

FEARLESS PRINCIPLE: *Cultivate reverence for God*

Prepare to serve God by cultivating reverence for him. God told Satan that Job was a man who "fears God and stays away from evil." This fear refers to respect, admiration, and love. It's not a cringing trepidation, but a reverential awe. Proverbs 8:13 reminds us that this fear involves hating evil, pride, arrogance, corruption, and perverse speech. To say it another way, reverence for God is the beginning of wisdom.[7]

Looking at Isaiah 6, we get a sense of what this reverence looks like. Isaiah describes a vision in which he saw God, who was high and lifted up. This vision caused Isaiah to feel undone; he was awed by God's majesty and felt completely sinful in the presence of God's consummate holiness. He experienced reverential awe.

This reverential awe includes hating evil. How often we find ourselves *avoiding* evil but still being strangely drawn to it. Most of us have some daring sin characterized as "the sin that so easily trips us up."[8] I find myself wanting to do wrong things in spite of my ministerial calling. But when we develop reverential awe, we will actively avoid and even flee from evil—just as we would run from a monster. Perhaps if Lot had developed a greater aversion to sin, he would not have chosen the region of Sodom and Gomorrah as a place to live. As we begin to see sin from heaven's perspective, we find evil nauseating and revolting. To thrive fearlessly in a threatening world, we must go from tolerating sin to abhorring it.

Job's reverential awe manifested itself in his integrity. God described him as "blameless—a man of complete integrity."[9] This integrity refers to how he aligned his actions to match God's standard of righteousness. Job did not deviate from God's requirements. He obeyed God with passion and cultivated reverence for the divine.

FEARLESS PRINCIPLE: *Prepare to serve*

With regard to Job, God asked the devil, "Have you noticed my servant Job?"[10] To prepare for God to use you in a dangerous world, learn to see yourself as a servant. Paul writes, "This is how one should regard us, as servants of Christ and stewards of the mysteries of God."[11] This servant mentality helps us focus more on what we can contribute to our world than on what we can take from it. It also empowers us to make pleasing God our primary motivation. Paul puts it this way in his letter to the Colossians: "Do your work willingly, as though you were serving the Lord himself, and not just your earthly master. In fact, the Lord Christ is the one you are really serving, and you know that he will reward you."[12]

During my days as a naval officer, I repeatedly received a blessing by thinking of God as my employer. No matter who my commanding officer was, I thought of God as the one who evaluated my labors. I found that this perspective affected what time I arrived at work and left. It influenced how long I took my lunch breaks and how I interacted with people. It motivated me to raise my standards, to go the second mile. To prepare for the Kingdom work that God has chosen for us in the midst of a threatening environment, make service a priority.

FEARLESS PRINCIPLE: *Submit to God's providence*

Job submitted to God's providence. He greeted the most devastating news with declarations of faith. When he learned of his children's deaths, he declared, "The Lord alone gives and takes. Praise the name of the Lord!"[13] Life sometimes confronts us with unpleasant experiences, but we can trust God even when we don't understand why bad things seem to happen to good people.

The Old Testament character Joseph is a classic example of someone who submitted to God's providence. In spite of many setbacks, Joseph refused to complain or blame God. During life's most bitter seasons, he maintained excellence in his work and outlook. It took thirteen years for Joseph to go from being cast into a pit by his fratricidal brothers to becoming the second most powerful man in Egypt. Nonetheless, he accepted the unfolding of God's powerful providence with calmness and equanimity, thereby thriving fearlessly in a threatening world.

FEARLESS PRINCIPLE: *Make family a top priority*

Job made family a top priority. He was the priest of his household, regularly praying for his children. Even when his wife suggested that he curse God and die, he maintained his faith.[14] Preparing to be used by God requires that we excel at home. Once after Jesus cast a demon from a man, the healed worshiper wanted to follow him. But Jesus challenged him with these words, "Go home to your family and tell them how much the Lord has done for you and how good he has been to you."[15]

Making family a top priority may mean putting aside other important things. Jacob made family a top priority. In Genesis 33, Esau offers to travel with his brother, but Jacob thought about his family and gave this response: "Master, you know traveling is hard on children, and I have to look after the sheep and goats that are nursing their young. . . . Why don't you go on ahead and let me travel along slowly with the children, the herds, and the flocks."[16] Jacob slowed down for his family. Those aspiring to be selected by God for service should do the same.

FEARLESS PRINCIPLE: *Strengthen your prayer life*

Job found blessings and power in prayer, and so can we. Alfred Lord Tennyson declared that "more things are wrought by prayer than this world dreams of."[17] When we love God, we desire to communicate with him. The best way to do so is through prayer. Jesus often spent all night in prayer. If he made prayer such an important priority, perhaps we should do likewise. When faced with impending death, he spent long hours praying in the garden of Gethsemane.

Elijah is another Bible character who made a commitment to prayer. James reminds us that even though Elijah was human like we are, his passionate prayers stopped the rain for three and a half years.[18] Elijah didn't waver in his prayer life. As the drought persisted, he prayed for rain seven times, persevering even when no clouds appeared, until God answered him.[19]

FEARLESS PRINCIPLE: *Develop your God-given talents*

With David, we learn the importance of developing our talents in order to be used by God in a dangerous world. David killed Goliath with one stone from a slingshot. David did not develop such precise hand-eye coordination without practice. He sharpened his God-given talents.

In the New Testament, Jesus tells a parable about a man who went on a long trip, leaving three servants in charge of his estate in his absence.[20] When he returned, he called his servants to account for the portion of the estate they each had managed. Two of the servants had invested and developed what was entrusted to them, and each returned a profit, earning the master's praise. The third servant had buried what he was given in the ground and had nothing to show for his work. Instead of a reward, what he had been given was taken away from him and given to the others. If we're to thrive in a threatening world, we must make the most of the gifts and talents that has God given us.

FEARLESS PRINCIPLE: *Build a reserve supply*

In Matthew 25, we find the parable of the ten bridesmaids. Five of them are described by God as wise, and five are depicted as foolish. These women are alike in their employment, expectation, and equipment. Yet they differ in their *preparation*, teaching us the importance of preparing for life's crises.

The five wise bridesmaids not only had oil in their lamps, but they also had a reserve supply. The foolish ones had oil only in their lamps, which soon ran dry when the bridegroom was delayed. I fly frequently and carry a laptop computer with me. On long flights, my computer battery inevitably runs down, and I have to shut off my computer. On one flight I noticed that my seatmate's computer continued to run after my battery had died. This seemed strange since we had turned on our computers at the same time.

"What kind of computer do you have?" I asked him.

"I have the same brand you do," he responded.

"Then why does your battery last longer than mine?"

"I bring an extra one," he said, "and I change it when the first wears down."

If having a backup battery helps with computers, think of what we can accomplish if we keep a backup "spiritual battery," as the five wise bridesmaids did in Jesus' parable. Perhaps Peter is referring to such spiritual reserves when he offers this advice: "Do your best to improve your faith. You can do this by adding goodness, understanding, self-control, patience, devotion to God, concern for others, and love."[21] That sounds like a backup "ethical battery" to me.

FEARLESS PRINCIPLE:
Don't deplete your reserve resources

We learn from the five wise bridesmaids not to deplete our reserve resources if we want to measure up to God's high standards. Often, when we're seeking to accomplish a goal, other people's demands can distract us. In the parable of the bridesmaids, the foolish ones say to the wise ones, "Let us have some of your oil!"[22]

But the wise women answer, "There's not enough oil for all of us! Go and buy some for yourselves."[23] You see, there are spiritual resources we cannot afford to lend to others without jeopardizing our own eternal well-being. Sometimes we must say no, rather than permit others to deplete our irreplaceable spiritual resources.

Once while preparing for a military physical readiness test, I had to learn to say no to others so that I could focus more clearly on my goal. I was desperately trying to find time for the aerobic and resistance training necessary to score an "outstanding" on the test, but people kept interrupting my work. They were inviting me to dinner, asking for counseling, and presenting other considerations. To remain focused, I had to say no. In the same way, for spiritual pursuits we must learn to prioritize what we do to ensure that our ethical and moral reserves aren't depleted by well-meaning people.

FEARLESS PRINCIPLE: *Activate your backup*

The story of the five wise bridesmaids ends with their activating their reserved resources. When the bridegroom delayed his arrival, they had to use the oil in their reserve vessels. They activated their backup.

To thrive in a threatening world, we may have to draw on reserve resources. Jesus illustrated this by keeping his thoughts directed toward God and praying for several hours in the garden of Gethsemane the night before his death. You never know when you'll be forced to draw on reserve powers during a moment of physical, emotional, or spiritual testing. Those who want to be prepared to be used by God must learn to obtain, protect, and activate reserve spiritual resources. This will enable us to be in the world but not defiled by it.

Prepare to be chosen for service on God's team by following these principles:

- Cultivate reverence for God.
- Prepare to serve.
- Submit to God's providence.
- Make family a top priority.
- Strengthen your prayer life.
- Develop your God-given talents.
- Build a reserve supply.
- Don't deplete your reserve resources.
- Activate your backup.

PURPOSEFUL PRAYER

God of our fathers and mothers, may we never forget how you have sustained us in the past. Help us prepare for active service in your Kingdom. Give us the wisdom to trust you in the small things, realizing that faithfulness with little prepares us for fidelity with much. May we trust you to do what is best for our lives in good times and in bad. We place our hope in your mighty name. Amen.

CHOOSE RESCUE
OVER RUIN

I AM FASCINATED by history books written from the perspective of *what if*? What if the confederacy had won the Civil War or Lincoln had not been killed? What if Hitler had prevailed or Japan had won the Battle of Midway? What if Jesus had not been born? What if?

This fascination with *what if* can be seen in Frank Capra's classic movie *It's a Wonderful Life*, starring Jimmy Stewart. In the movie, Stewart plays George Bailey, a man overwhelmed by financial challenges, who considers ending his life. Rescued from his suicide attempt by Clarence, a guardian angel, George is given a glimpse of what the world would have been like if he had never lived. He discovers that his life had indeed enriched humanity, contributing substantively to the well-being of many marginalized people and leaving the earth a better place than he had found it.

We sometimes feel the weight of living lives that matter. The challenge is exacerbated by the fact that we were conceived in sin and brought forth in iniquity.[1] Born with the congenital disease of sin, our urges and desires torture us like two headstrong horses pulling in opposite directions.

✗ When I was growing up, I became angry at the perceived unfairness of being labeled a sinner at birth before I'd even had a chance to commit a single sin, all because of what Adam had done. The fact that "in Adam all die" seemed to me a grave injustice.[2]

Later, I discovered that Paul gives the solution in the very same sentence in which he identifies the problem: "Even so in Christ all shall be made alive."[3] And he expands on this point in his letter to the Romans: "Just as through the disobedience of the one man the many were made sinners, so also through the obedience of the one man the many will be made righteous."[4] This meant that my standing with God changed because of Calvary, making me a saint even before I manifested a single bit of righteous fruit in my life. That, too, is unfair, but it's an injustice that makes me rejoice. Our standing with God through Christ is not based on our obedience, but on the obedience of Jesus. This is God's glorious rescue plan. He enables us to go from ruin to rescue, thereby allowing us to live fearlessly in a threatening world.

We should strive to go from ruin to rescue because we're born in sin. No one has to teach us to lie, cheat, or steal; we're good at these misdeeds without taking a single lesson. The apostle Paul writes, "I know that nothing good lives in me, that is, in my sinful nature. I want to do what is right, but I can't. I want to do what is good, but I don't. I don't want to do what is wrong, but I do it anyway."[5] We know from experience the truth of Paul's struggle, for we daily wrestle with our own tendency to sin.

In spite of the many flammable areas in our lives that can be ignited by the sparks of temptation, if we adhere the following principles, we can go from ruin to rescue and live fearlessly in a threatening world.

FEARLESS PRINCIPLE: *Know sin's endgame*

Going from ruin to rescue begins with understanding sin's endgame: "The wages of sin is death, but the free gift of God is eternal life through Christ Jesus our Lord."[6] Sin's endgame is our complete ruin. Romans 5:14 puts it this way: "Everyone died—from the time of Adam to the time of Moses—even those who did not disobey an explicit commandment of God, as Adam did. Now Adam is a symbol, a representation of Christ, who was yet to come."

Whenever we're tempted, we should remember that it's simply the devil's bait. Each time we're tempted to sin, we're playing a game of ethical Russian roulette; it's not worth the risk. James 1:15 says, "When sin is allowed to grow, it gives birth to death." When we understand this, we find motivation for cultivating a godly reverence that hates sin, pride, arrogance, and evil.[7]

FEARLESS PRINCIPLE: *Accept God's rescue plan*

We can also go from ruin to rescue because God has already put a plan in place to salvage our lives. As Ephesians 2:8-9 reminds us, "God saved you by his grace when you believed. And you can't take credit for this; it is a gift from God. Salvation is not a reward for the good things we have done, so none of us can boast about it." We should gratefully accept this salvation as a free gift.

Once while on a speaking engagement in the Virgin Islands, my wife and I charged our expenses to our room as we enjoyed the pleasures of that tropical paradise. Though we spent somewhat cautiously, uncertain as to how much of our expenses would be covered by our host, we reasoned that it was a once-in-a-lifetime opportunity to create some blissful memories.

The day of reckoning finally came when we had to check out of the hotel. As I waited for the desk clerk to hand me the bill for our five-day stay, I fully anticipated an exorbitant total.

When I received the bill, I could hardly believe my eyes. Stamped across the bottom line were the words, *Paid in full.* The people who had invited my wife and me had covered *all* of our expenses. As I stood there, incredulous, I caught a microcosmic glimpse of the joy we'll experience when we fully grasp the truth that Jesus has already paid the price for our salvation.

As we seek to thrive in a dangerous world, we must remember that Christ's obedient life not only *makes* us clean, but also *keeps* us clean. Our standing with God is not altered by our mistakes and missteps, for our debt has been paid in full by the life of our blessed Savior.

FEARLESS PRINCIPLE:
Acknowledge God's initiative in our salvation

The amazing thing about God's rescue is that he initiated it long before we were interested in him. Romans 5:10 says, "If, while we were God's enemies, we were reconciled to him through the death of his Son, how much more, having been reconciled, shall we be saved through his life!"[8] We receive salvation because of God's mercy. He loved us even when we were unlovable. The dying thief at Calvary learned this lesson, crying out to Jesus for salvation at the eleventh hour and finding it.[9] We, too, can be the recipient of a similar grace— but let's not wait until the eleventh hour!

This amazing grace comes to us because of God's initiative. What Jesus said to his disciples applies to all believers: "You didn't choose me. I chose you."[10] How great is his mercy in taking this initiative. John reminds us that we come to God only because he has drawn us to himself.[11] How astonishing it is that we don't even *want* to do what's right without special help from God, who works to give us "the desire and the power to do what pleases him."[12]

FEARLESS PRINCIPLE: *Celebrate God's great love*

Romans 5:8 tells us what motivated God to bless us with this rescue plan: "God showed his great love for us by sending Christ to die for us while we were still sinners." God's love for humankind caused him to send his Son to save us, not to condone or condemn our sins.[13]

Growing up, I attended church nearly every week, and I remember well a hymn we used to sing, titled "Love Lifted Me."

I was sinking deep in sin, far from the peaceful shore.
Very deeply stained within, sinking to rise no more.
But the Master of the sea heard my despairing cry.
From the waters lifted me, now safe am I.

Love lifted me! Love lifted me!
When nothing else could help,
Love lifted me.[14]

Like the prodigal son's father, who gave unconditional love to his returning backslidden son, so God saves us even though we don't deserve it. He brings us from ruin to rescue and empowers us to live fearlessly in a dangerous world.

FEARLESS PRINCIPLE:
Depend on God's abounding grace

The wonderful thing about God's rescue plan is that it even leaves us margin for error: "God's law was given so that all people could see how sinful they were. But as people sinned more and more, God's wonderful grace became more abundant."[15] God's rescue plan is like giving a financially challenged individual $10 billion in a bank account to cover a $10,000 debt. The debtor could never live long enough to spend the deposit made by the beneficent benefactor. God's rescue plan is built on his abounding grace, and we can't give more than God, no matter how hard we try.

Our standing with God has been secured through the obedience of his Son, enabling us to live fearlessly in a threatening world. We can thrive by following these positive principles:

- Know sin's endgame.
- Accept God's rescue plan.
- Acknowledge God's initiative in our salvation.
- Celebrate God's great love.
- Depend on God's abounding grace.

PURPOSEFUL PRAYER

Eternal Father, our souls long for you, for we find strength and joy in your presence. Increase our faith and teach us to trust you, even during life's storms. When we endure dark nights of the soul, may we find strength and joy in your presence. We claim your promise that you will never leave us or forsake us, and that nothing can separate us from your love. Help us to seek, in every undertaking, to know your will. Amen.

THRIVE
IN A PREDATORY WORLD

---✦---

7

PUNCTUATE YOUR LIFE WITH PURPOSEFUL PRAYER

WHEN I WAS YOUNG, my mother gave my siblings and me five cents for each Bible verse we memorized. This motivated us to look for the "low-hanging fruit" of short verses, and we found a treasure trove in 1 Thessalonians 5:

> "Rejoice evermore."[1]
> "Quench not the Spirit."[2]
> "Despise not prophesyings."[3]
> "Abstain from all appearance of evil."[4]

I loved these terse, money-making verses. But 1 Thessalonians 5:17 not only earned me a nickel, it also left me with a question. The text says, "Pray without ceasing." Three simple words, but what could they possibly mean? I pondered the question: Is it possible to pray nonstop? Is it possible to bathe our moments, days, months, and years continuously in prayer?

As I grew and matured spiritually, I began to believe it *is* possible to cultivate a spirit of habitual devotion, keeping our hearts attuned to God's transcendence and immanence. The Greek word translated as "without ceasing" in 1 Thessalonians 5:17 is *adialeiptos*, which means "constantly recurring" or "regular." In other words, we can punctuate our moments with regular intervals of recurring prayer.

Ralph Waldo Emerson, the American essayist, brought some clarity to this theme in his essay titled "Pray Without Ceasing," in which he made the following observation: "It is not only when we audibly and in form, address our petitions to the Deity, that we pray. We pray without ceasing. Every secret wish is a prayer. Every house is a church, the corner of every street is a closet of devotion."[5]

To illustrate further, while in college, I fell in love with the woman I eventually married. That romantic experience helped me better frame this biblical command to pray continuously, to punctuate one's life with prayer. I knew intuitively that it's possible to love without ceasing, for the presence of one's beloved produces recurring adoration. For me, that adoration has continued unabated for decades. Likewise, adoration for God can enable us to be continuously aware of his presence, creating a desire to punctuate our days, hours, and minutes with the communion and fellowship of prayer. This adoration can transform sporadic and stammering prayers into a continuous attitude of reverence and dependence on God.

I remember fondly an old 1950s Jimmy Stewart movie called *Harvey*. Stewart plays Elwood P. Dodd, an eccentric bachelor who interacts constantly with an imaginary six-foot-three-inch rabbit named Harvey. Throughout the movie, Stewart's character is aware that he is engaging unceasingly with his imaginary friend.

The eternal God is not imaginary. The glory of the sunrise and the majesty of the sunset remind us that he is alive and well. He inspires us to punctuate our lives with joyful and recurring communication with him.

Yes, it's possible to keep our minds consciously in God's presence. Perhaps this is what the psalmist was suggesting when he declared, "I will bless the Lord at all times; his praise shall continually be in my mouth."[6] This may also be what the prophet Isaiah is attempting to emphasize when, in referring to God, he says, "You keep him in perfect peace whose mind is stayed on you."[7]

How then can we punctuate our lives with purposeful prayer to better prepare ourselves for dealing with a dangerous world?

FEARLESS PRINCIPLE: *Pray with adoration*

Do you pray with purpose? Purposeful prayer involves adoration. Your prayers should begin with worship that lifts praises to God. That is adoration. How would you feel if you were a parent whose child spoke to you only when he or she wanted something? In contrast, how would you feel if that child strove to nurture a warm and loving relationship with you? God desires that we come to him with adoration, not only when we want something, but also just because we cherish our relationship with him.

The psalmists often encourage us to give praise to God. In Psalm 148:7-13, we find this all-encompassing exhortation:

> Praise the Lord from the earth,
>   you creatures of the ocean depths,
> fire and hail, snow and clouds,
>   wind and weather that obey him,
> mountains and all hills,
>   fruit trees and all cedars,
> wild animals and all livestock,
>   small scurrying animals and birds,

kings of the earth and all people,
    rulers and judges of the earth,
young men and young women,
    old men and children.
Let them all praise the name of the LORD.
    For his name is very great;
    his glory towers over the earth and heaven!

In Psalm 150:6, the psalmist boils it down to a single phrase: "Let everything that breathes sing praises to the Lord!"

Do your purposeful prayers begin with adoration? Take a look at Nehemiah's prayer in Nehemiah 1:5-6: "O Lord, God of heaven, the great and awesome God who keeps his covenant of unfailing love with those who love him and obey his commands, listen to my prayer! Look down and see me praying night and day for your people Israel." Nehemiah wanted God to help his people rebuild Jerusalem's walls, but he didn't begin his prayer with that request. Notice how his prayer begins with adoration for God. Yes, Nehemiah knew how to pray with purposeful adoration.

FEARLESS PRINCIPLE: *Pray with confession*

Purposeful prayer includes confession. God is willing to forgive our sins, but we must ask him to do so.[8] Failure to confess our sins can keep God from listening to our prayers.[9]

Nehemiah included confession in his purposeful prayers. After expressing adoration to God, he says, "I confess that we have sinned against you. Yes, even my own family and I have sinned! We have sinned terribly by not obeying the commands, decrees, and regulations that you gave us through your servant Moses."[10]

Nehemiah wasn't the only biblical character to confess national sins. Look at this prayer from Ezra: "O my God, I am utterly ashamed; I blush to lift up my face to you. For our sins are piled higher than our heads, and our guilt has reached to the heavens."[11] Ezra knew that purposeful prayer includes confession.

How often do you confess your sins to God? After the 9/11 tragedy, I participated with Bill Bright in a National Solemn Assembly at Constitution Hall in Washington, DC. During that service, scores of Americans confessed our nation's sins to God, petitioning him to heal our land. This was a great reminder to keep confession as an important part of our purposeful prayers.

FEARLESS PRINCIPLE: *Pray with supplication*

Purposeful prayer includes supplication. Supplication simply means earnestly talking to God about our needs and wants. We can get a better feel for supplication by looking again at Nehemiah's prayer. After he expresses his adoration for God, he continues with an earnest expression of need: "Please grant me success today by making the king favorable to me. Put it into his heart to be kind to me."[12]

Nehemiah worked for King Artaxerxes and needed to request help for rebuilding Jerusalem's walls. That's what he wanted God to do for him, and he requested it as his only petition in this purposeful prayer. But he preceded this request with adoration and confession.

Is something bothering you that you should talk to God about? Philippians 4:6 says, "Pray about everything."

When I was living in South Carolina, someone offered me a job in Florida. Unsure about what to do, I took the matter to God. "Lord," I said, "this seems like a good opportunity, but I don't know what the future holds. If you want me to accept the offer, let me see twenty-five Florida car tags tomorrow, right here in Beaufort, South Carolina." Well, someone must have been having a convention for Floridians in Beaufort the next day because everywhere I drove I saw Florida tags. God answered my prayer.

I almost didn't pray about that particular job offer. I felt that God probably had better things to do than to be concerned about my vocational decisions. Then I remembered the verse in Philippians: "Pray about everything." It helped me to believe that whatever concerned me was an appropriate prayer issue that I could talk to God about.

Do you have issues that you should be bringing to God in prayer? Are there challenges in your life that you're attempting to bear alone? First Peter 5:7 admonishes us, "Give all your worries and cares to God, for he cares about you." When we give our burdens to God, we also must *leave* them with him. Sometimes we're tempted to give our cares to God, but then we take them back as we say amen. He wants to bear our burdens, so anything that bothers us can be handed to him.

FEARLESS PRINCIPLE: *Pray with submission*

Those who pray purposefully surrender to God's agenda. They pray with submission. He is the potter, and we're the clay. "Does a clay pot argue with its maker? Does the clay dispute with the one who shapes it, saying, 'Stop, you're doing it wrong!'"[13] Of course not! If God is sovereign, why not submit to his will and his agenda?

We should submit with passionate delight. King David declares, "I take joy in doing your will, my God, for your instructions are written on my heart."[14] The knowledge that God desires the best for our lives should motivate us to delight in his guidance, leaning not on our understanding, but deferring to his providence.[15] This God-honoring submission will surround us with the shield of God's love.[16]

Even Jesus submitted to the Father's agenda. In the garden of Gethsemane, he stared into the cup of suffering and recoiled. He had already confided to his disciples, "My soul is crushed with grief to the point of death."[17] Therefore, he cried out to his Father in passionate prayer: "If it is possible, let this cup of suffering be taken away from me."[18] This was not, however, the end of his prayer, for he quickly added, "Yet I want your will to be done, not mine."[19]

What did God's agenda entail for his Son? Jesus would be despised and ridiculed by the religious leaders, denied and betrayed by Peter and Judas, forsaken by his other disciples, insulted by Caiaphas, teased by Herod, patronized by Pilate, brutalized by soldiers, cursed by dying felons, and ridiculed by a rapacious mob. That was God's agenda, a journey that led past Calvary through an empty tomb and back to heaven, a plan that ended in triumph.

Throughout this ordeal, Jesus prayed with submission. His last words before dying were "Father, into your hands I commit my spirit!"[20]

The purpose of prayer is not to persuade a reluctant deity, but to give God permission to give us his best for our lives. He didn't make us robots; he made us free moral agents. God gave us the power and freedom to say *no* to him, something he didn't give to the animals. But when we go to God in prayer, trusting in his providence and submitting to his will, he directs our paths, providing us with his best for our lives. "No good thing does he withhold from those whose walk is blameless."[21]

We can punctuate our lives with purposeful prayer by doing the following:

- Pray with adoration.
- Pray with confession.
- Pray with supplication.
- Pray with submission.

PURPOSEFUL PRAYER

Our Father in heaven, thank you for the opportunity to punctuate our lives with purposeful prayer. With our intercession, we sing of your steadfast love and proclaim your faithfulness to all generations. Today, strengthen us to walk in the light of your countenance. Abide with us so that your wisdom will influence each decision we make. Guide us past the pitfalls that lead to ruin. Empower us to glorify you in all we say and do and to live fearlessly in a dangerous world. Amen.

8

BREAK THE DEVIL'S GRIP

I'VE NEVER RECEIVED a call like it, before or since. I was summoned to the hospital to pray for a young man who had been shot in the face and was grotesquely disfigured.

"Pray for my child, Chaplain," begged his mother, though he was already brain-dead.

Knowing there was little hope for his survival, the mother timidly asked me, "If he dies, will you deliver the eulogy at his funeral?"

I didn't even know her son, but I agreed to speak at the memorial service, hoping to bring some comfort to the family. When I received the news that he had been pronounced dead, I prepared my funeral sermon from the passage in Matthew 13, where Jesus tells the story about a farmer who plants good seed in a field, but when harvest time arrives the farmer finds that weeds have come up with the wheat. When his servants ask how the harvest could have been compromised, the farmer responds, "An enemy has done this!"[1]

Like it or not, we must face the fact that an enemy is loose in our dangerous world. With predatory intentions, he "prowls around like a roaring lion, looking for someone to devour."[2] We're told in Ephesians 6:12 that "we are not fighting against flesh-and-blood enemies, but against evil rulers and authorities of the unseen world, against mighty powers in this dark world, and against evil spirits in the heavenly places." A predatory enemy is alive and active on planet Earth.

Jesus confirmed the existence of a real devil when he said to his disciples, "I saw Satan fall from heaven like lightning!"[3] So perhaps we should stop thinking that psychological disorders are primarily due to biological imbalances or environmental influences. Perhaps we should at least admit that psychological problems may also occur because a rapacious enemy seeks to bring destruction to our world. Perhaps it's time to acknowledge the reality of the demonic realm.

In Mark 5:1-13, we find the story of Jesus' encounter with a demon-possessed man. Jesus had just calmed a storm on the Sea of Galilee, and upon reaching the far shore, he encountered "a man possessed by an evil spirit."[4]

"Then Jesus demanded, 'What is your name?' And he replied, 'My name is Legion, because there are many of us inside this man.'"[5]

A "legion" was a contingent of six thousand Roman soldiers, so when this victim of Satan told Jesus his name, he also provided information about the strength of Satan's power within him. Believing that Jesus had come to torment them before the judgment day, the demons appeared to be trying to intimidate Jesus. Undeterred by this declaration of superior forces, Jesus commanded the demons to leave the man, and they did, rushing into a herd of two thousand pigs feeding on a nearby hillside. The pigs promptly stampeded into the sea.

It's important for us to realize that Jesus has absolute power and authority over any and all demonic forces at work in the world. As we strive to break the devil's grip on our world, we can use the following strategic principles.

FEARLESS PRINCIPLE: *Seek to know the devil's devices*

Breaking the devil's grip on our lives requires knowledge of his satanic strategies. Hosea declares, "My people are destroyed for lack of knowledge."[6] In other words, a knowledge deficit can bring catastrophic consequences. But as Paul later says in reference to Satan, "We are not unaware of his schemes."[7]

What do we need to know about the demonic realm? We need to know and remember that Satan is a fallen angel with great power and experience. He once sought to overthrow God's celestial government, declaring, "I will ascend to heaven and set my throne above God's stars."[8] But although he has the power of an angel, he doesn't possess the attributes of God, for he is not omnipotent, omniscient, or omnipresent. That's another way of saying that Satan isn't all-powerful, all-wise, or capable of being everywhere at once. He can't read your mind or tell the future. He also has limited time to do his evil work.[9]

Perhaps the greatest hurdle he faces is when believers pray. In Matthew 15, a mother comes to Jesus pleading for her demon-possessed daughter. On the strength of the mother's intercession, Jesus heals the girl. Similarly, in Matthew 17, a father brings his demonized son to Jesus. And even in spite of the father's weak faith, Jesus heals the boy. When we cry out to God on behalf of those who are shackled by addictions and spiritual bondage, he often answers our prayers by delivering those for whom we have interceded.

But far more important than our intercession are the prayers of Jesus on our behalf. He is the great intercessor.[10] Speaking to Peter shortly before his betrayal, Jesus said, "Satan has asked to sift each of you like wheat. But I have pleaded in prayer for you, Simon, that your faith should not fail. So when you have repented and turned to me again, strengthen your brothers."[11]

Imagine that. Jesus prays for us. Jesus knew that Peter would fail, denying the Lord three times in one night. Nevertheless, he interceded with the Father on Peter's behalf, believing passionately in the power of his prayers to extricate Peter from satanic control. Jesus didn't say to Peter, "*If* you repent," but "*When* you have repented." Our prayers, and the prayers of Jesus on our behalf, help people break the devil's grip on their lives.

FEARLESS PRINCIPLE:
Understand the root of satanic bondage

Our spiritual bondage is rooted in our divided nature. We were born in sin and shaped in iniquity, conceived by sinful mortals.[12] Our divided makeup has been appropriately described by Plato, who said the human will is like two headstrong horses pulling in opposite directions. The apostle Paul knew about the bondage of our divided personalities. In Romans 7:18, he observes, "I know that nothing good lives in me, that is, in my sinful nature. I want to do what is right, but I can't. I want to do what is good, but I don't. I don't want to do what is wrong, but I do it anyway."[13]

Sigmund Freud, a pioneer in human psychology, divided the psyche into three parts: *id, ego,* and *superego*. The id consists of the urges of the flesh, the superego comprises our ethical and moral yearnings, and the ego attempts to bring harmony between the two. Freud would likely agree with the demoniac: We are legion; we are many.

In Luke 18, a rich young ruler goes to Jesus determined to walk a righteous path. "Good teacher, what must I do to inherit eternal life?" he asks.[14]

Jesus responds, "Sell everything you have and give to the poor, and you will have treasure in heaven. Then come, follow me."[15] This admonition was too challenging for the divided personality of the wealthy young ruler, and he left Jesus with great sorrow. To break the devil's grip on our lives and remain fearless in a predatory world, we must understand that he will try to divide and conquer, but Jesus calls us to be integrated in all aspects of our personality.

FEARLESS PRINCIPLE: *Anticipate satanic intimidation*

To break the devil's grip, we should also expect to encounter satanic intimidation. Satan is a bully. His declaration to Jesus regarding the name Legion was an unsuccessful attempt to intimidate the Savior. In Luke 9:42, the devil throws a boy onto the ground and ravages him in response to Jesus' command that the demon should depart. When attempting to break the grip of the enemy, we can expect a fight.

Fortunately, even minimal resistance will reveal that we are dealing with a bully. James 4:7 puts it this way: "Humble yourselves before God. Resist the devil, and he will flee from you." As a young man, when I first sought to resist Satan's overtures, I expected the mother of all wars to ensue, but it didn't happen. Like most intimidators, he started running at the first sign of my resolve.

FEARLESS PRINCIPLE:
Expect to be pushed out of your comfort zone

If you want to break the devil's grip on your life, expect Jesus to push you out of your comfort zone. When he healed the demoniac called Legion, he allowed the demons to go into two thousand pigs that were grazing on a hillside. These pigs immediately dashed over a cliff into the sea, destroying the wealth of their owners. When the herdsmen and other people in the town saw this, they asked Jesus to leave, for he had pushed them out of their comfort zone, disrupting their lives and commerce. They seemed to care more about their loss of property than about the restored man who sat near Jesus, fully clothed and in his right mind.

In John 4, when Jesus moves to break the devil's grip on the life of the woman at the well, he pushes her out of her comfort zone.

"Go and get your husband," Jesus told her.

"I don't have a husband," the woman replied.

Jesus said, "You're right!" You don't have a husband—for you have had five husbands, and you aren't even married to the man you're living with now."[16]

By forcing the woman to confront the pathology in her life, Jesus enabled her to break the devil's grip on her destiny.

Perhaps this penchant for pushing people out of their comfort zones is what Simeon is referring to in Luke 2:34-35 when he prophesies about the baby Jesus: "This child is destined to cause many in Israel to fall, and many others to rise. He has been sent as a sign from God, but many will oppose him. As a result, the deepest thoughts of many hearts will be revealed." This prophecy came true, and Mary standing beside the cross as her son was crucified may have remembered the ominous words of Simeon: "A sword will pierce your very soul."[17]

Being a follower of Jesus guarantees that we will face opposition. "Everyone who wants to live a godly life in Christ Jesus will suffer persecution."[18] Moreover, "Your enemies will be right in your own household!"[19] Nonetheless, we can stay fearless in a threatening world.

FEARLESS PRINCIPLE: *Trust the authority of Jesus*

The surest way to break the devil's grip on your life is to trust the authority of Jesus. Demons are intimidated by the sound of Jesus' name; they are well aware of God's might and tremble at the thought of an approaching day of judgment.[20] In Matthew 8:29, they ask Jesus, "Have you come here to torture us before God's appointed time?" Unnerved by Jesus, they beg him to cast them into the herd of swine.

Imagine that. Angels who once inhabited eternity and sang anthems around the throne of God were reduced to begging Jesus to send them into a herd of pigs. They were filled with terror in the presence of Jesus.

In Luke 10, the disciples learn how demons are held hostage to Jesus' authority. Returning from a missionary journey, they excitedly inform Jesus, "Lord, even the demons obey us when we use your name!"[21] Jesus responds, "I saw Satan fall from heaven like lightning! . . . But don't rejoice because evil spirits obey you; rejoice because your names are registered in heaven."[22] Jesus knew that the power of his name could break the devil's grip, even when it was spoken with the delegated authority received by the disciples.

FEARLESS PRINCIPLE:
Continue to trust when God says no

When the crowd that gathered saw that the pigs had all drowned in the lake, they asked Jesus to leave their town, and he agreed to go. But when the healed demoniac asked Jesus if he could go with him, Jesus said, "No, go home to your family, and tell them everything the Lord has done for you."[23] Jesus had a reason for refusing this man's request, and this new follower of Jesus had to learn to take the Lord at his word.

Similarly, we must continue to trust Jesus, even when he says no to our requests. This was the level of trust that enabled Job, in the midst of all his suffering, to cry out, "God may kill me, but still I will trust him."[24]

Like Job, Martin Luther had a similar resolve to trust God, even when he didn't understand God's ways. In his grand hymn, "A Mighty Fortress Is Our God," he writes, "And though this world, with devils filled, should threaten to undo us, we will not fear, for God hath willed His truth to triumph through us. The prince of darkness grim, we tremble not for him; his rage we can endure, for lo, his doom is sure. One little word shall fell him."[25]

FEARLESS PRINCIPLE:
Use your testimony of deliverance to bless others

Our freedom from the devil's grip should motivate us to share our testimony of deliverance with others. Perhaps this is what Paul is referring to when he says, "The God of all comfort . . . comforts us in all our troubles, so that we can comfort those in any trouble with the comfort we ourselves receive from God."[26]

The woman at the well in John 4, newly freed from her bondage to sin, went home and said to the townspeople, "Come and see a man who told me everything I ever did!"[27] She wanted others to experience the comfort she had received from Jesus. In response, "the people came streaming from the village to see him."[28] What a blessing to be able to help others receive the comfort that Christ has given us.

We all can be free from bondage to sin and evil by not being ignorant of the devil's devices. We should neither overestimate nor underestimate our enemy, who is far more experienced than we are but does not possess omnipotence, omniscience, or omnipresence—which are attributes belonging only to God. As we strive not to be intimidated by evil, even when pushed out of our comfort zones by our mighty Savior, let us trust the authority of Jesus' name to break the demonic shackles and keep us walking in freedom. Then with Martin Luther, we can say, "Though devils all the world should fill, all eager to devour us. We tremble not, we fear no ill; they shall not overpower us."[29]

We can break the devil's grip in a dangerous world by doing the following:

- Seek to know the devil's devices.
- Understand the root of satanic bondage.
- Anticipate satanic intimidation.
- Expect to be pushed out of your comfort zone.
- Trust the authority of Jesus.
- Continue to trust when God says no.
- Use your testimony of deliverance to bless others.

PURPOSEFUL PRAYER

Beautiful Savior, free us from our bondage to evil. You have been our dwelling place in all generations, sustaining us with your steadfast love. Surround us today with the shield of your divine protection and favor, enabling us to resist the devil so that he will flee from us. Teach us to obey your commands, doing your goodwill, as we find joy in your presence. Keep us from doing those things that would bring us regret, remorse, and shame. Renew our strength as you provide us with the courage to carry on. Amen.

9

PASS LIFE'S TESTS

AS I SETTLED INTO MY SEAT in the classroom and realized we were having a pop quiz, I felt blindsided. I had not yet read the most recent chapter assignment, nor had I anticipated this sudden evaluation of our mastery of the class material. I looked around the room and noticed the usual suspects, the best students, looking confident. But for me, "judgment day" had arrived most unexpectedly.

Life is many things. It's a race to be run, a battle to be fought, and a test that we must pass. And sometimes when we least expect it, God gives us a pop quiz. Abraham didn't anticipate that God would ask him to sacrifice Isaac on the altar.[1] But he passed the test nonetheless. Esther didn't anticipate having to risk her life to save her people.[2] But she, too, passed the test. David didn't expect to encounter the giant Goliath in the valley of Elah, but the young shepherd passed the test.[3] Are you preparing yourself to pass life's pop quizzes, midterms, finals, and even makeup exams? Or are you about to be blindsided?

Why should we strive to pass life's tests? First, because a sinful and cruel world makes it necessary. The world is not a friend to those who seek to live godly lives. In fact, the apostle Paul tells us we all will "suffer persecution."[4] If we're living to honor God, we can expect tribulation just as Jesus said: "Here on earth you will have many trials and sorrows."[5] If godliness is not one of our goals, we will still encounter tests because even "the way of the unfaithful is hard."[6] So whether we're godly or ungodly, we should prepare ourselves for a life of tests, for these are the slings and arrows of outrageous fortune to which we are heirs, as we strive to stay fearless in a threatening world.

A second reason we should strive to pass life's tests is because they precede our eternal reward of a crown of righteousness. Paul talks about the blessing in 2 Timothy 4:7-8: "I have fought the good fight, I have finished the race, and I have remained faithful. And now the prize awaits me—the crown of righteousness, which the Lord, the righteous Judge, will give me on the day of his return. And the prize is not just for me but for all who eagerly look forward to his appearing." Paul says that life is a battle to fight, a race to win, and a faith to safeguard. In other words, life brings tests, and we must be prepared. The reward for passing these tests is a crown of righteousness, something far better than anything the world may offer. This crown is reserved not only for Bible patriarchs, prophets, and heroes of the faith, but also for ordinary people like you and me. This should motivate us to live fearlessly in a threatening world.

A third reason why we should strive to pass life's tests is because God often uses them to prepare us for greater service. Just as passing the PhD oral exams qualifies doctoral candidates to write their dissertations and be considered experts in their fields, the tests of life are sometimes necessary prerequisites before God can give us greater responsibility.

In some ways, we're like an automobile being tested before certification. On the test course, these vehicles are driven at speeds far faster than permitted on normal highways. They are exposed to wear and tear that no normal driver would ever think of allowing, for the manufacturers have a standard they're seeking to meet. Vehicles that can't measure up to the high standard don't make it to the showroom to be sold.

Often in the Bible, we see testing as a prelude to greater usefulness. In Luke 22:32, Jesus prepares Peter for such a time with these words: "I have pleaded in prayer for you, Simon, that your faith should not fail. So when you have repented and turned to me again, strengthen your brothers." In response, Peter asserts that he is ready to go to prison—or even die—in service to Christ.[7] But instead of congratulating his disciple's boldness, Jesus tells him precisely when the faith-testing trial would come: "Before the rooster crows tomorrow morning, you will deny three times that you even know me."[8] Like many of us, Peter was one major mistake away from really being useful to God for significant service. He still needed to learn that relying on our own strength—and all good intentions—isn't enough to carry us through. We need the power of God working in us and through us. But after Peter was thoroughly humbled by his failure—and repented—God was able to use him on the day of Pentecost not only to strengthen his brothers, as Jesus had called him to, but also to bring three thousand people into the Kingdom.[9]

But that was later. At the time Jesus responded so forcefully to Peter, this brash and vocal disciple was something of a legend in his own mind. Yet that very night, he would repeatedly fail his tests, experiencing the bitter pain and regret that would prepare him for greater service.

Even though Jesus knew that Peter would fail his tests, he still had confidence in him. The words *"when* you have repented," not *if,* should have given Peter some encouragement as he went out and wept bitterly because of his failure to live up to his boast: "Even if everyone else deserts you, I never will."[10]

Here's what we must do to prepare to pass life's tests.

FEARLESS PRINCIPLE: *Expect to be tested*

We should never think that just because we have accepted Jesus as our Savior that our trials have been permanently banished. Far from it. "How frail is humanity! How short is life, how full of trouble!"[11]

The apostle Peter, who faced his share of testing, writes, "Dear friends, don't be surprised at the fiery trials you are going through, as if something strange were happening to you."[12]

When we remember that our difficulties aren't unusual, that others must deal with the same challenges, it helps us to greet success and failure with the same calm resolve. We shouldn't be surprised when painful seasons come. We should *expect* them. Jesus expected to be tested. He "began to tell his disciples plainly that it was necessary for him to go to Jerusalem, and that he would suffer many terrible things at the hands of the elders, the leading priests, and the teachers of religious law. He would be killed, but on the third day he would be raised from the dead."[13] He was prepared to endure testing in a dangerous and predatory world.

If the purest person who ever lived was tested, we should also expect our share of trials. Perhaps Jesus came to expect tests because of his encounter with Satan in the wilderness.[14] Immediately after his baptism, "Jesus was led by the Spirit into the wilderness to be tempted there by the devil."[15] The Greek word for "tempted" here is *peirazein*, which actually refers to *testing* more than it does to *tempting*. It is what God did with Abraham in Genesis 22 when he commanded the patriarch to offer Isaac on the altar of sacrifice—a command that tested Abraham to his limit. But it was a *test*, not a temptation, for God would never seek to seduce anyone to do evil.

When God sent his Son to be tested, Jesus passed with flying colors, three times defending himself with Scripture, quoting from the book of Deuteronomy. After he passed his wilderness tests, the Bible records, "the devil left him."[16] But Jesus knew that his enemy would return; he *expected* future struggles.

FEARLESS PRINCIPLE: *Be faithful in the little things*

The success that Jesus had in passing life's tests teaches us a second lesson: We must be faithful in the little things. Though we know little about Jesus' early years, enough evidence exists to demonstrate his faithfulness in the little things. Before he confronted Satan in the wilderness, he lived at home for thirty years and was obedient to his parents.[17] Luke tells us that Jesus "grew in wisdom and in stature and in favor with God and all the people."[18] In other words, he developed intellectually, physically, spiritually, and socially.

Luke 16:10 tells us, "If you are faithful in little things, you will be faithful in large ones. But if you are dishonest in little things, you won't be honest with greater responsibilities." How we handle life's seemingly inconsequential things provides a window into our readiness for greater responsibilities. The fact that Rebekah possessed a vigorous work ethic, providing water for all of Abraham's servant's camels, opened the door for her to become Isaac's wife and the daughter-in-law of Abraham.[19] Little things matter for those who pass life's seasons of testing.

Another great example is Daniel, who prayed three times a day with clock-like precision.[20] He was so dependable and predictable with his prayers that his enemies used his fidelity to trap him, sending him to certain death in the lion's den. God, however, rewarded Daniel's faithfulness by protecting him from the ravenous beasts, shutting the mouths of the lions and keeping Daniel unharmed.

FEARLESS PRINCIPLE: *Practice self-denial*

To pass life's tests, we must also practice self-denial. As Jesus said to his disciples, "If any of you wants to be my follower, you must give up your own way, take up your cross, and follow me."[21] Are you ready to practice self-denial? Jesus demonstrated his own self-denial by fasting for forty days before his encounter with the devil in the wilderness.

Throughout the Bible, we meet people who passed life's tests because of a willingness to delay gratification and to deny themselves. Hananiah, Mishael, and Azariah refused to bow to Nebuchadnezzar's idol, and Daniel chose to be thrown into the lion's den rather than obeying an unjust law by King Darius.[22] Many more scriptural examples could be given about people who denied themselves to pass life's tests. It seems the cross precedes the crown.

We can prepare to pass life's tests by doing the following three things:

- Expect to be tested.
- Be faithful in the little things.
- Practice self-denial.

PURPOSEFUL PRAYER

Almighty God who inhabits eternity, whose throne is heaven and whose footstool is the earth, you have given us the gift of another day. May we never forget that we borrow our heartbeats from you. Continue to sustain us, and give us this day all that we need to glorify your holy name. Help us to be faithful in the little things to qualify for greater service in your Kingdom. Lord, make us poor in misfortune and rich in blessings. Give us enough challenges to keep us humble, enough hurt to keep us humane, enough failure to keep our hands clenched tightly in yours, and enough success to make us certain we are walking with you. We bless your mighty name. Amen.

BE AS WISE

AS A SERPENT

———— ✦ ————

SUCCEED IN SLIPPERY PLACES

WHY IS IT THAT SOME PEOPLE overcome the same temptation that overwhelms others? Joseph was able to resist sexual sin, but David gave in.[1] Ananias and Sapphira gave in to greed, but Abraham was generous with his wealth, giving his nephew Lot his choice of the land.[2] Why is it that some people are successful even in slippery places? They survive, and even thrive, despite being lambs in a wolf's world.

In 1 Chronicles 11:22-25, we meet Benaiah, one of King David's mighty men. This valiant soldier belonged to David's elite guard, who were legendary for their prowess and proficiency. Benaiah's claim to fame was that he killed a lion in a pit on a snowy day. It's impressive enough to kill a lion, as both Samson and David did,[3] but Benaiah's accomplishment is more impressive because he accomplished this feat in a pit on a snowy day.

He found success in a slippery place. How can we follow Benaiah's example and learn to succeed in slippery places?

FEARLESS PRINCIPLE: *Expect God to protect you*

You and I can find successes in life's treacherous places because, first of all, God has promised that "no weapon forged against [us] will prevail."[4] On our journey through life, the devil brings against us every weapon he can find or form. Such weapons present dangerous and slippery challenges. People of faith, however, can find encouragement in God's promise that such weapons will not succeed; we can expect God to protect us.

When I served as a US Navy chaplain, I had a boss who tried to intimidate me. "Barry," he said, "I don't like you, and I'm going to do my best to make sure you don't get promoted. If I'm ever on a promotion board, I want you to know that you're dead in the water. Your upward mobility is finished." Fortunately, God protected me from slipping into worry about his threats or concern about my career, and the years flew swiftly by without incident. Eventually, the day came when the man who had made these threats found himself working for *me*, and I was the one writing *his* evaluations. And just as God had protected me from my enemy's unfair taunts and threats, he now protected me from stooping to revenge or retribution against my adversary. Through it all, with faith in God, I learned that we can face the dangerous weapons of our enemies.

FEARLESS PRINCIPLE:
Believe that God will turn your negatives into positives

We can find success in slippery places because God can turn life's negatives into positives. Romans 8:28 assures us that "God causes everything to work together for the good of those who love God and are called according to his purpose for them." Repeatedly throughout Scripture we see people of faith experiencing God's power to transform negatives into positives. God took the negative of Adam and Eve's transgressions and turned it into a positive with a divine plan of salvation. He took the envy that King Saul had against David and turned it into the music of psalms. God has enabled countless people throughout history to find success even in dangerous places.

FEARLESS PRINCIPLE: *Trust God's promises*

We can find success in slippery places because God has promised that we will not miss out on any of his goodness. Psalm 34:10 tells us, "Even strong young lions sometimes go hungry, but those who trust in the Lord will lack no good thing." What an incredible promise. Often when we sin, it's because we are afraid of missing out on something special. We slip into transgression because of insufficient faith in God's promises. One of his greatest promises is found in Psalm 84:11: "The Lord will withhold no good thing from those who do what is right." We can trust God even when we can't trace him; we're not going to miss out on any of his goodness.

I believed that God wanted me to become a minister, but I ran from this calling. I didn't want to become a minister because all the preachers I knew were poor. I felt that my childhood of poverty was enough impoverishment to last for several lifetimes. "Lord," I cried, "I don't want to be a poor preacher." During my third year of college, I gave in reluctantly and began to pursue a theology major. I have been a minister now for more than forty years, and God has prospered me both spiritually and materially beyond anything I could have imagined. When you decide to serve and trust God, you won't miss out on your good thing.

FEARLESS PRINCIPLE: *Have confidence in God's love*

We can find success in slippery places because God will not permit anything to separate people of faith from his love—"neither death nor life, nor angels nor principalities nor powers, nor things present nor things to come, nor height nor depth, nor any other created thing, shall be able to separate us from the love of God which is in Christ Jesus our Lord."[5] God loves you and me with an incomprehensible and unconditional passion. The immensity of his love is described well in the the hymn "The Love of God" by Frederick M. Lehman: "Could we with ink the ocean fill, and were the skies of parchment made, were every stalk on earth a quill, and every man a scribe by trade, to write the love of God above would drain the ocean dry; nor could the scroll contain the whole, though stretched from sky to sky."[6] We must never doubt God's love. It is far too grand to ever fail.

I began to appreciate God's love on a more personal level after I became a father in 1978. When my first son was born, I marveled at the unconditional love I immediately felt for him. Seconds after his birth, I would have been willing to die for him, and that realization startled me. It dawned on me that, if I, with all my deficiencies, could experience such unconditional love for a newborn child, then God's love for me must be even more amazing. He sustains us in the slippery places of a dangerous world because of his amazing love for us. He enables us to say, "We're still standing, even though the world often threatens our security."

FEARLESS PRINCIPLE: *Accept God's guidance*

We can stand secure in slippery places because God will provide us with guidance through his Word. The psalmist Asaph writes, "You guide me with your counsel, and afterward you will take me into glory."[7] If we stumble and fall in the slippery places, we are without excuse because we have the advantage of godly guidance. Isaiah tells us, "Whether you turn to the right or to the left, you will hear a voice saying, 'This is the road! Now follow it.'"[8]

We can expect to receive guidance from God as we travel along life's labyrinthine pathways. Some months before the US Navy was to consider more than 160 captains for a single opportunity for promotion to admiral, I felt a powerful intuition that I should drive from Virginia Beach to Washington, DC, to set my military records in order. This intuition seemed illogical because I had already straightened out my records the previous year. I argued with myself; I didn't have time to waste on an unnecessary four-hour drive. But when I finally gave in to that nagging feeling and headed for DC, I found out that the military was moving from a paper system to a computerized one and that many service records had been compromised in the process. My records, in particular, were in shambles. I believe that my intuition was no accident and had a providential force behind it. By heeding that "still, small voice," I was able to rectify what could have been a catastrophe, and I was rewarded with the promotion to admiral.

Remember the story of the three magi in Matthew 2? They were deceived by King Herod, who said to them, "Go to Bethlehem and search carefully for the child. And when you find him, come back and tell me so that I can go and worship him, too!"[9] The wise men found the Christ child, but they disobeyed the king and returned home by a different route. They did this because God spoke to them in a dream and told them not to return to Herod. Let godly guidance help you find success in a dangerous world.

FEARLESS PRINCIPLE: *Don't envy the wicked*

We sometimes slip when we see the prosperity of wicked people. They, too, seem to be able to find success in slippery places. Psalm 73:2-3 declares, "As for me, I almost lost my footing. My feet were slipping, and I was almost gone. For I envied the proud when I saw them prosper despite their wickedness." Have you ever wondered why people who don't love or respect God still appear to do very well?

When I was growing up in the inner city of Baltimore, it seemed that the wicked prospered immensely. The drug pushers, prostitutes, and pimps seemed to be the ones with the fancy clothes, the big cars, and the unlimited cash. The gang members seemed to be the ones who walked fearlessly into the shadows. My family and I were going to church, singing hymns, and praising God, and still we were poor, while the wayward among us seemed to flourish like green trees. It's a slippery slope and enough to tempt us to deviate from our integrity.

How then did I remain upright in that slippery and dangerous environment? Along with Asaph the psalmist, I found the right perspective through worship: "When I thought how to understand this [the prosperity of the wicked], It was too painful for me—Until I went into the sanctuary of God; Then I understood their end."[10] As I worshiped God in his sanctuary several times each week, I began to see that all that glitters isn't gold. I began to appreciate God's wisdom and see the underbelly of success that God hadn't endorsed.

In Isaiah 6, the prophet finds himself in a slippery place. His friend and mentor, King Uzziah, had died, smitten by God in judgment. Uzziah's death sobered Isaiah, and he soon caught a glimpse of God through a vision of heaven. In the presence of God's holiness, Isaiah felt unclean until one of the praising angels took a hot coal from God's altar and touched Isaiah's lips, purifying them. The prophet then heard God's voice reverberating in the corridors of his spirit: "Whom shall I send, and who will go for us?"[11] This question from God warmed Isaiah's heart, challenging him to make a commitment.

Isaiah said, "Here I am! Send me."[12] This worship experience helped Isaiah find the right perspective. No longer was he confused about God's justice as it related to the death of his hero, King Uzziah. Isaiah caught a glimpse of God's sovereignty through worship, and he was ready to become an instrument to be used for God's glory. Isaiah was standing in a slippery and dangerous place but was steadied and encouraged by the unfolding of God's loving providence.

Those who want to remain upright in slippery places should remember that success without God is no success at all. As Jesus himself inquires of us, "What do you benefit if you gain the whole world but lose your own soul?"[13]

Nebuchadnezzar, king of Babylon, discovered the futility of success without God. Standing on the balcony of his palace, he declared: "Is not this great Babylon, which I have built by my mighty power?"[14] This arrogant assertion offended God, bringing his judgment to bear on the king. Nebuchadnezzar spent the next few years away from his throne, living like a lunatic and eating grass like an ox. He learned that success apart from God is failure.

FEARLESS PRINCIPLE: *Stay near to God*

Perhaps the primary key to finding success in slippery places is to stay near to God. After Asaph talks about nearly losing his footing because he envied the prosperity of the wicked, he utters these words to God: "Those who are far from you will perish; you destroy all who are unfaithful to you. But as for me, it is good to be near God. I have made the Sovereign Lord my refuge; I will tell of all your deeds."[15]

The apostle Peter had success in a slippery place because of his nearness to God. In Matthew 14, he asks Jesus for permission to walk on water, and it is granted. As long as Peter keeps his focus on Jesus, he does the impossible, promenading on the waves. But as soon as he notices the boisterous winds, he becomes afraid and begins to sink. He cries, "Save me, Lord!"[16] And Jesus does. He reaches out and steadies Peter, and they walk back to the boat together.

Few places in our lives will be as slippery or as dangerous as the raging sea on which Peter walked with Jesus. That same Jesus is alive and well today, and he is willing to be a companion to you and me for all the days of our lives. As recorded in the book of Hebrews, he said, "I will never leave you nor forsake you."[17] He also said, "Lo, I am with you always, even to the end of the age."[18] You'll never have to walk alone again, not even in the valley of the shadow of death, for God will be with you, comforting you with his rod and staff, and causing goodness and mercy to pursue you.[19]

In the musical *My Fair Lady*, there is a wonderful song called "On the Street Where You Live." A young man named Freddie, who is pursuing a young lady named Eliza, is unable to get her to talk to him. Nonetheless, he is happy to be on the street where she lives, thrilled by the knowledge that she is near. How wonderful it would be if we had a similar passion for God.

David had such a passion. In Psalm 27:4, he writes, "One thing I ask of the Lord—the thing I seek most—is to live in the house of the Lord all the days of my life, delighting in the Lord's perfections and meditating in his Temple." Of all the things David desired, nothing surpassed his eagerness to be in God's presence. This should not surprise us, for the Bible says that in God's presence "there is fullness of joy."[20] We're also told that "[God] will keep in perfect peace all who trust in [him], all whose thoughts are fixed on [him]."[21]

Why are some people more successful in slippery places than others? I believe it's because some take advantage of the blessings God has promised to the faithful and follow his blueprint for success in a threatening world. The following principles will help direct your steps in staying upright in a dangerous world:

- Expect God to protect you.
- Believe that God will turn your negatives into positives.
- Trust God's promises.
- Have confidence in God's love.
- Accept God's guidance.
- Don't envy the wicked.
- Stay near to God.

PURPOSEFUL PRAYER

Nearer, still nearer, close to thy heart;
Draw me, my Savior—so precious Thou art!
Fold me, O, fold me close to Thy breast;
Shelter me safe in that "Haven of Rest."[22]

Our Father, you don't make promises to forget them or flit from
interest to interest, from friend to friend, or from love to love.
You, O God, with steadiness and perseverance move in the lives
of humanity. Awaken us to your inescapable presence so that we
will keep our minds on you. Enable us to feel your nearness as we
grapple with the problems of our earthly pilgrimage. We trust in
your merciful name. Amen.

FIND DELIVERANCE
FROM DISTRESS

I WAS STUCK IN TRAFFIC on the 14th Street Bridge in Washington, DC, and the winds of distress were blowing at me. I needed to be at the Capitol Building by 10 a.m., but at 9:45 I was still languishing on the bridge, crawling along at five miles an hour. Meanwhile, I rehearsed the worst-case scenario in my mind: *The CSPAN 2 cameras are rolling; the Senate president pro tem glances anxiously at the clock and the door, wondering where the chaplain is and who will offer the opening prayer. He certainly isn't prepared to offer an extemporaneous prayer with a few million people viewing him on television.*

The thoughts taunted me with the terrible shame of my situation. In my mind's eye, I saw lawmakers inquiring as to my whereabouts and attempting to determine whether the US Senate could still convene—with or without a prayer. Or would they have to cast lots for someone to perform the duty? I had no backup intercessors, no designated hitter; I was simply facing a phenomenon that life can frequently send our way: distress.

What is distress? It's a painful situation, a state of desperate need. Usually, it is accompanied by worry, particularly as one's troubled heart imagines the worst. Distress is a state of danger in which we must deal with something that seems to threaten the security of our tomorrows. Those who desire to remain fearless in a dangerous world must find deliverance from distress.

I usually spend most of my commute from northern Virginia to the US Capitol Building in prayer. But few things will focus a time of intercession quite like being stuck in a traffic jam caused by multiple accidents and knowing there's nothing you can do. Miraculously, I made it to the Senate chambers on time that day—but please don't ask me how. As I walked to the podium to deliver my invocation right on time, my heart was overwhelmed with gratitude and contrition, and my prayer that morning reflected those emotions.

As long as we're still breathing, we will go through seasons of distress, for "in this world you will have trouble."[1] God desires to deliver us from our distressful situations in order to empower us to comfort others with the comfort we have received from him.[2] Galatians 6:2 challenges us to "share each other's burdens, and in this way obey the law of Christ." We are expected to reach out to those in need, assisting them in extricating themselves from distress. In short, we're blessed in order to be a blessing.

Helping those in distress is one of the distinguishing marks of discipleship. "Your love for one another will prove to the world that you are my disciples," says Jesus.[3] Notice that it's not our rhetoric, but our actions, that provide unmistakable evidence that we are people of faith.

Therefore, not surprisingly, our willingness to help those in distress will provide the standard for conduct on Judgment Day. In his teaching about the judgment in Matthew 25:31-46, Jesus says that he will be interested in what has been done for the least, the last, the lonely, and the lost. Did we feed the hungry, provide water for the thirsty, clothe the naked, visit the sick, reach out to the incarcerated, and succor the strangers in our midst?

So how can we find deliverance from distress and stay fearless in a dangerous world?

FEARLESS PRINCIPLE: *Take your distress to God in prayer*
The first step for finding deliverance from distress so that we can remain fearless in a predatory world is to take the challenge of our distress to God in prayer. In fact, the more distress we encounter, the more alive and vibrant our prayer life should be. David puts it this way: "Answer me when I call to you, O God who declares me innocent. Free me from my troubles. Have mercy on me and hear my prayer."[4]

Many scholars believe that David prayed this prayer when he was being pursued by his son Absalom. Absalom had overthrown David's kingdom with a military coup. The preceding psalm, Psalm 3, is clearly connected to David's problems with Absalom, making Psalm 4 appear to be a continuation of David's prayer regarding that predicament. The beautiful thing is that David made prayer his first option; he immediately turned his heart to God. We would deal more effectively with our distresses by following his example.

God desires for us to call on him in our distress. He says, "Call on me when you are in trouble, and I will rescue you."[5] God won't get upset because we come to him only after we've reached the end of our hoarded resources or made prayer our fifth or sixth option. God stands ready to help us, ready to hear us, just when we need him most. To be delivered from our seasons of distress in a dangerous world, we must go to God in prayer.

FEARLESS PRINCIPLE:
Speak the truth boldly to your enemies
If we're living right, we can expect to make enemies, but we must learn to speak the truth boldly to them. This is exactly what David

does in Psalm 4: "How long will you people turn my glory into shame? How long will you love delusions and seek false gods?"[6] David wasn't timid about letting his enemies know that he would not be intimidated by their shenanigans. Later, the apostle Paul echoes David's resolve, instructing young Timothy to fire up his faith and his gifting: "God has not given us a spirit of fear and timidity. . . . So never be ashamed to tell others about our Lord."[7]

Like David, Nehemiah knew how to speak boldly to his enemies. When he was attacked as he attempted to rebuild Jerusalem's walls, he responded wisely. When his enemies said, "Come and let us meet together," Nehemiah refused to take the bait. Sidestepping their efforts to distract him, he responded with these words: "I am doing a great work and I cannot come down. Why should the work stop while I leave it and come down to you?"[8] Those who will find deliverance from distress in dangerous times must learn not to be turned aside by their enemies.

When David faced his enemy Goliath, he spoke boldly to the giant:

> You come to me with a sword, spear, and javelin, but I come to you in the name of the LORD of Heaven's Armies—the God of the armies of Israel, whom you have defied. Today the LORD will conquer you, and I will kill you and cut off your head. And then I will give the dead bodies of your men to the birds and wild animals, and the whole world will know that there is a God in Israel! And everyone assembled here will know that the LORD rescues his people, but not with sword and spear. This is the LORD's battle, and he will give you to us![9]

Don't be afraid to speak boldly to your enemies, for God will keep you strong and courageous in a threatening world.

FEARLESS PRINCIPLE: *Experience sanctification*

Sanctification means being set apart for holy use. Those who would find deliverance from distress should experience sanctification. Psalm 4:3 tells us, "You can be sure of this: The Lord set apart the godly for himself. The Lord will answer when I call to him." Again, David refused to be threatened by distressful situations, buoyed by the knowledge that he was special, set apart, and sanctified by God himself.

When was David set apart by God? In 1 Samuel 16, God sends the prophet Samuel to David's family home to select Israel's next king, Saul's successor. David was God's choice, and the prophet anointed him with oil. Such special recognition could easily infuse us with a spirit of courage. After all, God's anointing on our lives ensures our survival until we have fulfilled his plan for our lives. That's why David could face Goliath with such courage.

As he did with David, God has anointed and set apart people of faith in our day. As the apostle Peter tells us, "You are a chosen people, a royal priesthood, a holy nation, God's special possession, that you may declare the praises of him who called you out of darkness into his wonderful light."[10] As a follower of Jesus, you are special. Allow the truth of your being set apart for God's holy purpose to keep you fearless in a dangerous world.

FEARLESS PRINCIPLE: *Commune with your heart*

To be delivered from distress, sometimes you must slow down and commune with your heart. As David advises, "Silently search your heart as you lie in bed."[11] This advice resonates with that given in James 1:19: "Be quick to listen, slow to speak, and slow to get angry." How often do you listen to your heart?

I learned about a Jesuit practice called the Daily Examen, which involves a self-examination exercise to do before you go to sleep. One abbreviated version is to think about what happened that day for which you are thankful, followed by an examination of the things you would do differently if you could. Finally, you simply resolve to improve on the things you would have done differently, falling asleep with greater peace because you have communed with your heart. I've begun to practice the Examen each night. It's a wonderful spiritual tonic.

FEARLESS PRINCIPLE: *Cultivate reverence and integrity*

Possessing reverential awe makes it easier to live with integrity. Psalm 4:4 declares, "Stand in awe, and sin not."[12] This same kind of awe is alluded to in Proverbs 1:7: "Fear of the Lord is the foundation of true knowledge." When we possess reverence for God, we are reluctant to displease him by sinning, for we begin to see sin as God sees it. That is why Proverbs 8:13 tells us that "all who fear the Lord will hate evil. Therefore, I hate pride and arrogance, corruption and perverse speech." We can gauge our level of spiritual fitness by how repulsive sin has become to us. If it still titillates, we still have work to do.

Joseph found sin so revolting that he said to Potiphar's wife when she tried to seduce him, "How could I do such a wicked thing? It would be a great sin against God."[13] For Joseph, the adultery that this woman proposed was more than an affair. He saw sin as God saw it, as a great wickedness, and chose instead—out of reverence for God—to resist temptation and live with integrity, even though his refusal put him in prison under a false charge of rape.

Do you hate sin as much as God does? Sin cost the life of our Savior, Jesus Christ. He paid much too high a price for us to trivialize our transgressions. Find deliverance from distress and stay fearless in a dangerous world by cultivating reverence and integrity.

FEARLESS PRINCIPLE:
Receive the gifts of gladness and peace

Two blessings come from being delivered from distress: the gifts of *gladness* and *peace*. We sometimes minimize these internal blessings, but they are as valuable as many external ones. The psalmist writes, "You have given me greater joy than those who have abundant harvests of grain and new wine. In peace I will lie down and sleep."[14] Gladness and peace are blessings worth coveting. How marvelous it is to know joy in the Lord as great as that of those who celebrate a bountiful harvest, coupled with a peace that passes understanding. This will enable you to lie down and sleep with confidence that your best life is yet to be. This is a path for fearlessness in a dangerous world.

FEARLESS PRINCIPLE: *Trust God with your future*

Find deliverance from distress by trusting God with your future. That's what Job did when he went through a season of travail. In spite of his grief and anguish, Job said this about God: "He knows where I am going. And when he tests me, I will come out as pure as gold."[15] David evinces a similar trust in God when he writes, "You alone, O Lord, will keep me safe."[16] No one can really be certain what tomorrow may bring. That's why we're admonished not to brag *or* worry about what lies ahead:

> Don't brag about tomorrow, since you don't know what the day will bring.[17]

> Don't worry about tomorrow, for tomorrow will bring its own worries. Today's trouble is enough for today.[18]

The truth is that our future is in God's hands.[19] When we trust him to deliver us from distress, we discover that he provides us with a security that the world can't give or take away. So how do we find deliverance from distress and stay fearless in a dangerous world? We follow these wise guidelines:

- Take your distress to God in prayer.
- Speak the truth boldly to your enemies.
- Experience sanctification.
- Commune with your heart.
- Cultivate reverence and integrity.
- Receive the gifts of gladness and peace.
- Trust God with your future.

PURPOSEFUL PRAYER

Holy Spirit, you deliver us from our distress. When we call you in our day of trouble, you align our lives with your wonderful will. You're the giver of every good and perfect gift. Eternal God, we are sinful people seeking salvation. We are lost people seeking direction. We are doubting people seeking faith. Show us the path to a meaningful life; reveal to us the steps of faith. Quicken our hearts and purify our minds, as you broaden our concerns and strengthen our commitments. Amen.

CONQUER FEAR

IN HIS 1939 CHRISTMAS DAY radio address, King George VI of England quoted an obscure British writer named Minnie Louise Haskins, a retired missionary and social science instructor:

And I said to the man who stood at the gate of the year:
"Give me a light that I might tread safely into the unknown."
And he replied:
"Go out into the darkness, and put your hand into the hand
    of God.
That shall be to you better than light and safer than a known
    way."[1]

Those who seek to stay fearless in a predatory world will need to find God's hand in the darkness.

In Matthew 2, the magi found God's hand in a dark and dangerous world. They had studied the starry heavens, exploring the mysteries of celestial bodies, and noticed when a luminous and strange light appeared. With exceptional faith, they embarked upon a journey, traveling mostly at night to an unknown destination. The desert winds blew as they traveled into the unknown, bringing their best gifts for a newborn king.

Reaching the land of Israel, they descended the Mount of Olives with Jerusalem in the distance. With eager steps they pressed forward, fixing their eyes on a guiding light. Finally, they reached Jerusalem and commenced their inquiry: "Where is he who has been born king of the Jews?"[2] Their arrival created quite a stir—of surprise, fear, and contempt. Nonetheless, these seekers, who had the courage to venture unafraid into the unknown, can teach us a valuable lesson about living fearlessly in a dark and threatening world.

What lessons can we learn from the magi about surviving in a dangerous world?

FEARLESS PRINCIPLE: *Stay open to new ideas*

A critical lesson to learn from the magi is to be open to new ideas. We will not stay fearless for long in a dangerous world if we close our minds to God's ongoing guidance and direction. The magi received light from God that the Jewish religious leaders missed. Divine illumination penetrated the darkness of heathenism, and astronomers seeking truth followed its brightness. The religious leaders in Jerusalem quoted Micah 5:2, demonstrating that they knew where Jesus would be born. Unfortunately, they lacked the experiential relationship with God that would prompt them to walk five miles to witness and worship the Messiah.

How tragic it is to think that we own a truth monopoly. We can become like the disciples in Mark 9:38, who said to Jesus, "Teacher, we saw someone using your name to cast out demons, but we told him to stop because he wasn't in our group."

"'Don't stop him!' Jesus said. 'No one who performs a miracle in my name will soon be able to speak evil of me.'"[3] In other words, keep an open mind about how God may choose to work in the world.

In John 10, Jesus makes a similar point: "I have other sheep, too, that are not in this sheepfold. I must bring them also. They will listen to my voice, and there will be one flock with one shepherd."[4] It's interesting that he doesn't say "I'll one day have these sheep," but instead, "I have other sheep [already]." They were already his children. This should motivate us to have greater tolerance for those who think differently than we do and reduce our certainty that our little group has the corner on all truth. Stay close to the Lord and keep an open mind to new ideas, and life may surprise you with what you might learn.

FEARLESS PRINCIPLE:
Trust God to guide you into the future

The second lesson of the magi is to trust God to guide you into the future. We often seem to forget that God already knows what will happen tomorrow, for he is all-knowing. In Luke 22, Jesus predicts Peter's denial down to the very moment—as the rooster crows. That's amazing. If Christ knew with such specificity how Peter's fall would occur, certainly he is wise enough to order our steps and choreograph our future. Job believed that God was guiding his future. He said, "He knows the way that I take; when he has tried me, I shall come out as gold."[5] And the last words of Jesus from the cross were, "Father, I entrust my spirit into your hands!"[6]

God has promised to guide us into the future—a future that he has laid out for us. "For we are his workmanship, created in Christ Jesus for good works, which God prepared beforehand, that we should walk in them."[7] In Proverbs, we're told: "Trust in the Lord with all your heart, and do not lean on your own understanding. In all your ways acknowledge him, and he will make straight your paths. Be not wise in your own eyes; fear the Lord, and turn away from evil.

It will be healing to your flesh and refreshment to your bones."[8] In other words, our future is in good hands when God is in control.

FEARLESS PRINCIPLE: *Cultivate an exceptional faith*

Hebrews 11:6 reminds us that faith is indispensable for pleasing God. We see this in the third lesson of the magi: Believe God with an exceptional faith. Think of how incredible it was for these people to travel into the unknown, oblivious of where they would finally stop.

"Honey, where are you going?" Perhaps one of the magi's wives asked this question.

"Sweetheart, I don't know where I'm going," he may have responded. "I'm simply following a star."

We see this kind of exceptional faith in Genesis 12:1 with the call of Abram. God says to this soon-to-be sojourner of faith, "Leave your native country, your relatives, and your father's family, and go to the land that I will show you."

Abram was seventy-five years old, but his faith was sufficiently exceptional that he obeyed, even though he didn't know where he was headed. Similarly, the magi left home simply following a star.

FEARLESS PRINCIPLE: *Develop spiritual discernment*

The magi provide yet a fourth lesson: the importance of developing spiritual discernment. Thousands of people saw the star in the heavens, but only the magi possessed sufficient spiritual discernment to follow it. Others who gazed at the heavens saw nothing supernatural, but the magi permitted the star to declare God's glory.

God often uses those outside the family of faith to do his work. In 1 Kings 17, we find Elijah, God's prophet, in a bit of trouble. The brook that had sustained him through years of drought had finally dried up, and it was time for him to move on. God spoke to him: "Go to Zarephath, which belongs to Sidon, and dwell there. . . . I have commanded a widow there to feed you."[9]

Jesus later observed that there were many widows in Israel at the time of Elijah, but God selected a foreigner of the same race and religion as the wicked queen Jezebel to feed his prophet.[10] This widow was selected partly because of her spiritual discernment. Though not an Israelite, she heard God's voice, and like the magi, she followed his leading in a dangerous world.

FEARLESS PRINCIPLE: *Find guidance in God's Word*

The magi, however, needed more than a star. Entering Jerusalem, they sought specific information about a coming king. Herod called his religious scholars together, and they quoted from Micah the prophet, pinpointing Bethlehem as the place for the birth of the Christ child.

This teaches us lesson five from the magi: Find guidance in God's Word. Second Timothy 3:16-17 reminds us that God's Word is "profitable for teaching, for reproof, for correction, and for training in righteousness."[11] In Matthew 4:4, Jesus observes that "people do not live by bread alone, but by every word that comes from the mouth of God." The magi were led to Bethlehem by the light of biblical prophecies that validated their experience.

Let God's Word guide your experience, as Jesus' disciples did. In Luke 5, after they had fished all night and caught nothing, Jesus showed up and said, "Put out into the deep and let down your nets for a catch."[12]

Peter responded, "Master, we toiled all night and took nothing! But at your word I will let down the nets."[13] Peter obeyed Jesus and caught so many fish that the nets began to break. Miracles can happen when we find our guidance in God's Word.

FEARLESS PRINCIPLE: *Expect trouble*

The sixth lesson of the magi is straight to the point: Expect trouble. "Life is short and sorrowful for every living soul."[14] The magi encountered serious trouble. Instead of Jerusalem rejoicing at their search, a cloud of anxiety and foreboding gripped the city from the palace to the shanty. King Herod was troubled and all of Jerusalem with him.

How nice it would be if we could sojourn through this world trouble-free. But it's just not going to happen. "Indeed, all who desire to live a godly life in Christ Jesus will be persecuted."[15] We can expect heartaches and disappointments in life.

When we expect trouble, we keep the devil from isolating us. Isolation can lead to despondency, prompting us to feel as if we're the only ones who must "suffer the slings and arrows of outrageous fortune."[16] Like Elijah in 1 Kings 19, we're sometimes tempted to think that we're the last survivor among the righteous—even if there are seven thousand saints we've overlooked. Expecting trouble reminds us that others are called to endure the same vicissitudes and hardships. This empowers us to hold on and persevere.

FEARLESS PRINCIPLE: *Live fearlessly*

When we realize that God is bigger than our problems, it should enable us to live without fear. But to *remain* fearless in a dangerous world, we must habitually eliminate fear from our lives.

We fear the future. We fear it partly because of anxiety about the unexpected and the unknown. The fact is, we rarely know what tomorrow may bring—joy or sorrow, peace or conflict. Proverbs 27:1 admonishes us not to boast about tomorrow because we "don't know what the day will bring." And James warns us not to say that "today or tomorrow we are going to a certain town and will stay there a year . . . do business there and make a profit."[17] For how do we know what will happen tomorrow?

In the waning days of 2007, the news media announced the assassination of Pakistani political leader Benazir Bhutto, who only recently had returned home after nine years in exile. Yes, the future is uncertain. Some time ago I preached in South Carolina and gave an invitation to discipleship. Several people responded to this call to accept Jesus as Savior and Lord, including a twenty-three-year-old man. Later at a potluck dinner, he informed me that he had delayed coming to Christ but felt that this might be his last opportunity for salvation. He was murdered the following Tuesday. Indeed, who knows what a day will bring forth?

I preached the young man's funeral, a celebration of a life covered by God's mercies. Despite the brevity of his life, this young man made the most important decision one can make: a commitment to Christ. I preached with joy, fully anticipating that I will see my new friend at the resurrection of the righteous who have died.[18]

In the early days of my military ministry, I ran to catch a helicopter that would fly me to different ships to conduct divine worship. On this particular day, I was detained by a sailor who had just received news of his mother's death. Someone on the ship's public address system bellowed, "Chaplain Black, if you're not on the flight deck in three minutes, your transportation will be unavailable." I said my final few words to the sailor and dashed with all the speed I could muster up the several flights of stairs to the flight deck, arriving just in time to see the helicopter leave without me. At first, I felt consternation, but it quickly turned to terror when—only minutes after taking off—the helicopter crashed, killing everyone on board except the pilot, who was seriously injured. Again I was reminded of the twists and turns that each day may bring.

The magi teach us that we can live without fear. In a dream, God told them to go home another way and not return to the murderous King Herod, who planned to kill Jesus. If God is that involved in the details of our lives so that he warns us in our dreams, it should reassure us that he orders our steps as well, protecting us from dangers seen and unseen.

One week before Pan Am Flight 103 was shot down over Lockerbie, Scotland, I took the same flight on the same plane. When I learned of the tragedy, it caused me to pause and reflect on life's fragility and God's hand in our lives. God knew when I would fly and which plane would crash, even as Jesus knew in advance which disciples would betray and deny him. God knows the way our paths will take us throughout life's seasons, and this should produce in us a calm assurance that all will be well.

Minnie Louise Haskins had it right. We can have something "better than light and safer than a known way" if we put our hands "into the hand of God." As we move into the unknown future, no fear should taunt us and no anxieties should deter us. God is greater than any enemy that waits behind the mist of the future. By his might, our best days beckon. So thrive in a threatening world by adhering to the following principles:

- Stay open to new ideas.
- Trust God to guide you into the future.
- Cultivate an exceptional faith.
- Develop spiritual discernment.
- Find guidance in God's Word.
- Expect trouble.
- Live fearlessly.

PURPOSEFUL PRAYER

Lord of the universe, help us to conquer fear. As we learn to live in day-tight compartments, show us duties left undone. Give us the desire to do your will so that we will remember vows unkept and tasks unattended. Lead us even through life's challenging seasons to a deeper commitment to you. Send us out to be your instruments of good in the world. Thank you for your promise that you will never leave us nor forsake us. We pray in your sacred name. Amen.

GIVE MORE WITH LESS

MOTHER'S DAY WAS THE NEXT DAY, and I didn't know what
to do. I was only eight years old, and I wanted to get my mother a
gift that told her how much I loved her. But I had one thin dime.
Meandering down to the neighborhood store owned by Mr. Katts, I
searched his shelves for something that would honor my wonderful
mother and cost no more than ten cents. After some time, I finally
settled on a box of wild cherry cough drops for a nickel and a small
box of Kleenex tissues, which also cost a nickel. *That's the ticket*, I
thought. For only a dime, I had two gifts that were sure to please
my mom.

When I returned home, my exuberance quickly turned to despair.
What a stupid gift to give someone, I thought forlornly. First, my
mother didn't even have a cold, so she really didn't need either gift.
Next, all I had for wrapping paper was the brown paper bag the store
owner had placed the items in. More to the point, I had four siblings

who would be certain to howl with laughter at my stupidity. What could I possibly have been thinking? Perhaps that was the problem— I hadn't been thinking at all. The anxiety I felt as I anticipated my humiliation the next day was palpable and painful.

The fateful hour arrived, and like a felon walking the green mile, I approached my mother's room with trembling trepidation and handed her the poorly wrapped gifts. I searched her face for some hint of approval but was unable to decipher her cryptic gaze. As she slowly opened the first gift, tears filled her eyes. Without looking at me, she proceeded to open the second package while I waited to exhale. Then my mother stretched her arms toward me and opened them wide.

"You're the best son any mother could possibly have," she whispered, drawing me tightly into her embrace and kissing the startled look from my face. Somehow, I had given more by giving less.

Looking back, I'm thankful I didn't decide not to give my mother a gift just because I thought I didn't have enough. Some gifts are worth far more than their market value simply because of the value added by the giver's motives. When we overcome our innate selfishness and give cheerfully, not grudgingly or out of necessity, the monetary value of the gift becomes secondary to our righteous motives.

In the Gospel of Mark, we find a story of well-motivated giving:

Jesus sat down opposite the place where the offerings were put and watched the crowd putting their money into the temple treasury. Many rich people threw in large amounts. But a poor widow came and put in two very small copper coins, worth only a few cents.

Calling his disciples to him, Jesus said, "Truly, I tell you, this poor widow has put more into the treasury than all the others. They all gave out of their wealth; but she, out of her poverty, put in everything—all she had to live on."[1]

Though she could have easily decided not to give anything, for the amount she possessed was a pittance compared to the other givers, this gracious and generous woman gave more by giving less. By giving out of her poverty and with pristine motives, she released everything she had to God. This act of courageous altruism pleased God more than the great sums given by all the rest, who gave but a fraction of their surplus. Like the cough drops and tissues that brought my mother great joy, this woman's paltry gift delighted God's heart.

How can we follow this woman's example and give more by giving less in a dangerous world?

FEARLESS PRINCIPLE: *Give with the right motivation*

We can give more to God by giving less when we give with the right *motivation*—which is more important than the amount. The apostle Paul expresses this truth in 1 Corinthians, where he writes, "If I gave everything I have to the poor and even sacrificed my body, I could boast about it; but if I didn't love others, I would have gained nothing."[2] That's an amazing verse. It says that without the motive of love, even the greatest gift is meaningless.

In 1 Kings 17, we find the prophet Elijah at a point of extremity. A famine has ravaged his country, for no rain has fallen for more than three years. Moreover, Elijah is a fugitive from justice, hunted like a wild animal by the most powerful man of his time, King Ahab. God miraculously sustained his prophet by a brook called Cherith and fed him with food brought by ravens. Suddenly, these provisions disappeared and the brook dried up. This posed no problem for God's power. He spoke to Elijah, saying, "Go to Zarephath, which belongs to Sidon, and dwell there. Behold, I have commanded a widow there to feed you."[3]

Zarephath had also been devastated by the long famine, and the widow to whom God sent Elijah was down to her last handful of flour and a few drizzles of cooking oil. When Elijah first meets her, she is out gathering sticks for a fire to prepare her last meal before she and her son will likely die of starvation. Nevertheless, she agrees to feed Elijah, out of the little bit she had left, before attending to her own needs. Though she wasn't an Israelite, she recognized the voice of God and stayed strong in dangerous times by giving more with less.

In the Gospel of Luke, Jesus commends this Old Testament woman's faith and generosity: "There were many widows in Israel in the days of Elijah, when the heavens were shut up three years and six months . . . and Elijah was sent to none of them but only to Zarephath."[4]

God honored the faithfulness of this widow in the land of Sidon, who gave more by giving less. She was supernaturally sustained for the rest of the famine because her motivation was obedience to God's command. Her motive was far more important than what she gave.

FEARLESS PRINCIPLE: *Give with the right attitude*

Motives are important, but so is *attitude*. One of the reasons God created free moral agents instead of automatons is because he wants his people to be volitional givers, people who give willingly. The apostle Paul writes, "Each one must give as he has decided in his heart, not reluctantly or under compulsion, for God loves a cheerful giver."[5] It's as if God is saying, "If you can't give with the right attitude, keep it."

Not long ago, I preached at a church where many in the congregation had the right attitude about giving. When the announcement for offering time was made, the congregation stood as one and applauded. It was one of the few times I've ever seen the collection of the offering receive a standing ovation. They were certainly cheerful givers.

FEARLESS PRINCIPLE: *Give in the right direction*

The *direction* of our giving is also more important than the amount. We must learn to give not primarily for this world, but for the world to come. Matthew 6:19-21 puts it this way: "Don't store up treasures here on earth, where moths eat them and rust destroys them, and where thieves break in and steal. Store your treasures in heaven. . . . Wherever your treasure is, there the desires of your heart will also be." If you want to know where someone's heart is, follow the money trail. Too many people talk a good game, but the direction of their gifts is more revealing. Are you investing for time or for eternity? The widow who gave so sacrificially that she earned Jesus' commendation was investing in eternity.

Why should we seek to invest for eternity? One good reason: "We brought nothing with us when we came into the world, and we can't take anything with us when we leave it."[6] Having officiated at more than three hundred funerals, I have yet to see a hearse with a luggage rack. Ownership is only an illusion.

This fact was driven home powerfully to me when I visited a home I had once owned. It had been my dream house, my pride and pleasure. I loved it so much that I would drive around the neighborhood, marveling that I had purchased something in such a beautiful area. The day came, however, when I sold it. When I later visited that city again, my old house drew me like a magnet. I drove to my old neighborhood, parked at a distance, and stared at the building that I had once called mine. Someone else's name was now on the deed; but the truth is, I had never really owned it. In fact, nothing I call mine can go with me beyond the grave, except perhaps my character.

But even though we "can't take it with us," we *can* send it on ahead—by investing in the lives of other people so that they, too, can live for eternity. I think of the many people who invested in my life who have since died—and yet their generosity continues to pay dividends. I think of a couple in my neighborhood, Al and Margaret, who would let me come to their home in the evening and experience a few hours away from the poverty and pathology of my own home. I lost track of what happened to them, but I will always be grateful for their unselfish and unconditional positive regard. The good in me today is partly due to the harvest of generous seeds they planted in me more than six decades ago.

FEARLESS PRINCIPLE: *Give sacrificially*

More important than the amount of the gift is the *cost* to the giver. Observing the contrast between the offerings given at the Temple by wealthy donors and the two copper coins that the widow dropped in, Jesus said, "They gave a tiny part of their surplus, but she, poor as she is, has given everything she had to live on."[7] Jesus wasn't impressed by the amount but rather the cost to the giver, for the widow gave her all.

I was once asked to speak for a chapel service at a school in Alabama. I didn't know the professor who had invited me, but he met me at the airport and drove me to his office. As I sat there, I saw a photograph he had of Martin Luther King Jr. that I had not seen before. It was a picture of him drinking coffee in an Alabama restaurant with a white man at a time when segregation was still legal. I asked my host, "Who is the man in the photograph with Dr. King?"

"That's my father," he responded. His father was an ethicist, who risked public scorn to do what he thought was right. His father watched some of his friends walk away from him, and he was shunned by some who thought he should follow the laws of segregation. He paid a high price for his integrity.

We see a similar generosity in the parable of the Good Samaritan.[8] On the road to Jericho, a priest and Levite pass by a wounded man in need of help, but a Samaritan risks his life to save the one victimized by violence. Perhaps Jesus was referring to such sacrificial service when he declared, "If anyone would come after me, let him deny himself and take up his cross and follow me."[9]

German pastor and theologian Dietrich Bonhoeffer was willing to pay the cost of discipleship. He lost his life fighting against the evils of Adolf Hitler's Nazi Germany. In his book *The Cost of Discipleship*, Bonhoeffer declares, "When Christ calls a man, he bids him come and die."[10] He knew that discipleship often requires us to pay a very high price.

The rich young ruler in Luke 18 was unwilling to pay that price.[11] He came to Jesus to ask for guidance about living the good life. Jesus responded, "Sell all that you have and distribute to the poor, and you will have treasure in heaven; and come, follow me."[12] The price was too high, and the young man went away sorrowful. Are you willing to pay the price to follow Jesus?

FEARLESS PRINCIPLE: *Give recklessly*

The amount of the gift is not as important as the *recklessness* of our giving. A marvelous recklessness characterized the gift of the widow. If you had two mites, why not give one and save the other for yourself? Why give it all?

Judas asked this question about Mary's gift of the alabaster ointment when he and Jesus attended a feast at the home of Simon.[13] When Mary entered and proceeded to bathe the Lord's feet with ointment that cost a year's wages, Judas asked, "Why did this woman waste so much? That money could have been used to feed the poor."[14]

Jesus responded vigorously to Judas's question: "Leave her alone! She has kept this perfume for the day of my burial. You will always have the poor with you, but you won't always have me."[15] Jesus endorsed Mary's memorable munificence, her reckless giving.

Perhaps the writer of Ecclesiastes was talking about righteous recklessness when he wrote, "Cast your bread upon the waters, for you will find it after many days."[16] Water seems an unpromising place to cast bread that you intend to eat. It seems so reckless. Yet this reckless giving carries with it the promise of a reward: "After many days you may receive a return."[17]

No one gave more recklessly than Jesus Christ. Dr. James Allan Francis notes this in his essay titled "One Solitary Life":

All the armies that ever marched, and all the navies that ever were built, and all the parliaments that ever sat, all the kings that ever reigned, put together have not affected the life of man upon this earth as powerfully as has that One Solitary Life.[18]

How reckless was his giving? The apostle Paul writes, "Though he was God, he did not think of equality with God as something to cling to. Instead, he gave up his divine privileges; he took the humble position of a slave and was born as a human being. When he appeared in human form, he humbled himself in obedience to God and died a criminal's death on a cross."[19] The Incarnation was a risky and dangerous undertaking. To break through at Bethlehem as a baby wrapped in swaddling clothes was at best a long-shot mission.

It was also reckless to leave the continuation of his operation to twelve contentious men, but that's what he did. His motivation was faultless, his attitude exemplary, his direction precise, his sacrifice incomprehensible, and his giving reckless. He stayed fearless and strong in a dangerous world.

Regardless of our material resources, we can give more by giving less in a threatening world by following these guidelines for giving:

- Give with the right motivation.
- Give with the right attitude.

- Give in the right direction.
- Give sacrificially.
- Give recklessly.

PURPOSEFUL PRAYER

God of light, in whom there is no darkness, teach us to give more even when we give less. Thank you for your guiding light that gently leads us. You're a mystery, but not a puzzle; profound, but not incomprehensible. You are loving, but not sentimental; patient and longsuffering, but not weak or indecisive. You are all things that we are not but need to be. Today, align our lives with your will. We trust you to choreograph our destinies in this dangerous world. We worship your holy name. Amen.

BE AS INNOCENT

AS A DOVE

---✦---

LIVE WITHOUT PRIDE

DURING THE NATIONAL BASKETBALL ASSOCIATION'S 2006 playoffs, Rasheed Wallace of the Detroit Pistons responded to a loss by guaranteeing that his team would win the next game. "Y'all can quote me. Put it back page, front page, whatever."[1]

But Wallace's Pistons didn't win the next game. His over-confidence went unrewarded as his team experienced back-to-back losses.[2] Living fearlessly in a threatening world involves avoiding the pitfalls of pride.

"Let anyone who thinks that he stands take heed lest he fall."[3] In this verse, Paul warns us about pride, a false confidence that leads us away from joy. We despise the sin of pride in others, but we often can't see it in ourselves. Pride is responsible for much of the world's chaos because it seduces us into thinking too highly of ourselves. Pride creates contention, hardens the heart against compassion, and encourages disdain of others. As it says in Proverbs 16:18, "Pride goes before destruction, and haughtiness before a fall." Failure to avoid pride is a key reason why many fail to thrive in a threatening world.

Eve, the first woman, failed to avoid the pitfalls of pride when she partook of the forbidden fruit. "She saw that the tree was beautiful and its fruit looked delicious, and she wanted the wisdom it would give her."[4] Eve desired a higher level of knowledge than God intended, and pride enabled sin to enter the world and infect humanity.

Rebekah made a similar mistake because of pride.[5] When it appeared that her son Esau would receive his father's birthright, she colluded with her other son, Jacob, to deceive her husband. Together, they tricked old-and-ailing Isaac into thinking that Jacob was actually Esau. The deception worked, but Rebekah's pride came at a painful price when Jacob was forced to flee from Esau, who was bent on getting revenge for what he had lost. Rebekah spent the rest of her life without Jacob's companionship, a victim of the destructive power of pride.

Even monarchs can become victims of arrogance and fail to thrive in a dangerous world. Once, a king named Herod permitted pride to destroy him.[6] A legend in his own mind, Herod decided to celebrate his reign on a special day. Arrayed in royal garments, he sat on his throne and spoke eloquently to the assembled throng, prompting them to shout: "It's the voice of a god, not of a man."[7] Herod accepted their praise without protest, thus sealing his doom. Suddenly, an angel from God struck Herod because he refused to give glory to God. In the end, this arrogant monarch was destroyed by pride and eaten by worms.[8]

Herod's tragedy teaches us that no one is immune to the destructive consequences of pride. It is an equal-opportunity destroyer, bringing down princes and paupers, annihilating clergy and laity alike. It takes down kings and presidents and ordinary people who think more highly of themselves than they should. Thousands stumble in life because of pride.

Herod's demise also reminds us of the importance of deflecting praise. Because our talents come from God, our Creator, we should redirect praise we receive to him. It's easy to say a simple, "I'm thankful that God helped you," to someone who praises us for a sermon we preached, a kind deed we performed, or other work we have done.

Herod's destruction also shows us how fragile our humanity is. Blaise Pascal once said, "Man is but a reed, the most feeble thing in nature, but he is a thinking reed. The entire universe need not arm itself to crush him. An exhalation, a drop of water, suffices to kill him."[9] Because we possess such fragile and temporary lives, we would do well to remember that we are sustained by a power greater than ourselves.

In 1963, businessman Howard E. Butt gave a speech he titled "The Art of Being a Big Shot," which provides some insight into the pernicious nature of pride.

> It is my pride that makes me independent of God. It's appealing to me to feel that I am the master of my fate, that I run my own life, call my own shots, go it alone. But that feeling is my basic dishonesty. I can't go it alone. I have to get help from other people, and I can't ultimately rely on myself. I'm dependent on God for my next breath. It is dishonest of me to pretend that I'm anything but a man— small, weak, and limited. So, living independent of God is self-delusion. . . . When I am conceited, I am lying to myself about what I am. I am pretending to be God, and not man. My pride is the idolatrous worship of myself.[10]

Those who seek to thrive in a threatening world must avoid the pitfalls of pride. As a primary source of conflict within families, between neighbors, and even among nations, pride is responsible for untold anguish in our world. Clinging to pride usually prolongs conflict.

Pride destroys the harmony and equilibrium that accompany the good life. Here are nine good reasons to avoid pride at all costs:

- Pride targets human weakness. Seldom are we as strong as we think.
- Pride can make temptations seem irresistible.[11]
- Pride leads to self-delusion. We may think we're spiritual giants when we're actually moral pygmies.[12]
- Pride makes us careless. The false confidence of pride can cause us to drop our guard. When David confronted Goliath in the Valley of Elah, the giant underestimated the young shepherd—a mistake that cost him his life.[13]
- Pride displeases God. In Amos 6:8, he says, "I despise the arrogance of Israel."
- Pride leads to inappropriate boasting. Sennacherib, the king of Assyria, made a premature and inappropriate boast to Hezekiah, the king of Israel. In the ensuing battle, Sennacherib was soundly defeated and Israel prevailed.[14]
- Pride plays a starring role in disagreements and contentions. "Pride leads to conflict; those who take advice are wise."[15]
- Pride hinders God's purposes. In Mark 6, when Jesus returns to his hometown, most of the people reject him. Their pride and lack of faith made it impossible for Jesus to do miraculous works among them, apart from a few healings.[16]
- Pride can lead to other sins. In 2 Samuel 11, King David brazenly commits adultery with Bathsheba *after* being told she was the wife of Uriah. This led to a cover-up that gave birth to other sins. David arranged the murder of Bathsheba's husband and then lived in hypocritical silence for nearly a year, until he was confronted by the prophet Nathan.[17]

So what can we do to resist pride in our lives?

FEARLESS PRINCIPLE: *Avoid the near occasion for sin*

Inevitably, sin has a prelude, an onset, a "neighborhood." Avoidance is often the first and best means to overcome temptation. In resisting the sinful overtures of Potiphar's wife, Joseph refused even to go near her.[18] Samson didn't avoid Delilah, and it led to his defeat.[19] Let me put it even more simply: If you have an alcohol problem, stay away from bars. If you have a pornography problem, filter the sites you're able to access online. Why subject yourself to unnecessary temptation? In Matthew 6:13, we're admonished to pray, "Lead us not into temptation."[20] In other words, Superman should stay away from kryptonite.

FEARLESS PRINCIPLE:
Refuse to compare yourself with others

In one of his letters to the church at Corinth, Paul writes, "We dare not class ourselves or compare ourselves with those who commend themselves. But they, measuring themselves by themselves, and comparing themselves among themselves, are not wise."[21]

If we look long enough, we can usually find someone who seems less faithful. Instead, look to the standards of the God who will one day judge us all, for we rarely have the right to judge others.

A good practice is to spend time reading about the life of Christ. His exemplary excellence dwarfs our efforts to live moral lives in our own strength. When we comprehend his passion for service and sacrifice, our efforts to measure up, flying solo, will cease. In fact, we will come to accept the reality that, without divine help, our personal strivings will inevitably fall short. Indeed, Jesus once said, "Apart from me you can do nothing."[22]

FEARLESS PRINCIPLE: *Get up immediately after you fall*

The essential difference between Judas and Peter can be seen in how they responded to their sin. Both betrayed Jesus, but Peter immediately repented. Judas hanged himself instead of seeking for-giveness. First John 1:9 encourages us to confess our sins to God—who is "faithful and just to forgive us." The moment we fall, we should come back to God in contrition, seeking the forgiveness he promises.

Occasionally, while I'm driving in DC rush-hour traffic, someone will nearly force me off the road or compel me to slam on my brakes, unleashing adrenaline and the fight-or-flight response. Usually, I control my temper. But sometimes I become so exasperated that I think or say something inappropriate. Without delay, I confess that sin to God.

FEARLESS PRINCIPLE: *Pursue humility*

Humility leads us away from pride. Humility is not groveling, but it involves an honest assessment of our God-given talents. It manifests itself in a teachable spirit. Like the newly converted Saul of Tarsus, we cry out, "Lord, what do You want me to do?"[23] Though conscious of successes, humility submits to correction. It moves us to repent, like Peter did after he had denied Jesus.[24] Humility helps us find the road to a life that matters.

FEARLESS PRINCIPLE: *Avoid contention*

One of the best ways to win an argument is to avoid it, for our dis-agreements are often rooted in pride. As Proverbs reminds us: "Too much pride causes trouble. Be sensible and take advice."[25]

When it comes to pride, we must prepare for ethical warfare. Ephesians 6:12 reminds us that our conflict isn't with flesh and blood, but with spiritual wickedness in high places, with princi-palities and powers. Such formidable opposition requires that we prepare for battle.

We can fight and resist pride by successfully following these guide-lines:

- Avoid the near occasion for sin.
- Refuse to compare yourself with others.
- Get up immediately after you fall.
- Pursue humility.
- Avoid contention.

PURPOSEFUL PRAYER

Lord of hosts, deliver us from arrogance and pride. Remind us that before honor comes humility and pride goes before a fall. Deliver us from the haughtiness that makes us legends in our own minds. Open our hearts to receive your Holy Spirit. Thank you for the promise to give your Holy Spirit to those who ask. Help us to bow to your will and live lives devoted to your providential leading. Bless our labor. Let faith, hope, and love abound in our lives. Use us to heal the hurt in our world. We pray in your majestic name. Amen.

15

LIVE WITHOUT LUST

AFTER PREACHING AT A CONVENTION, I met a talented minister and his family. They had picture-perfect good looks, gleaming smiles, and wholesome dispositions. The daughter looked like a high school cheerleader, and the son resembled the captain of a football team.

"Thank you for your powerful message, Chaplain Black," the pastor said as he shook my hand enthusiastically.

"Thanks for coming to worship," I responded. "I look forward to hearing your message during the evening service."

This congenial meeting made future events troubling. A few weeks later, the news broke. This friendly and gifted pastor had been asked to leave his prestigious church because of his acts of adultery.

"I don't believe it," I protested.

"It's true, Chaplain. Here's the newspaper article to prove it," said the friend who had brought me the news. And so it was.

Sadly, the media pounced all over this pastor's fall, sarcastically using King James English to describe the events that brought him down. With intonations of "We told you so," some journalists suggested that no clergy could be trusted.

As I read these news accounts, I began musing about what leads us to fall. Why had this gifted pastor permitted the trap of lust to destroy years of honorable labor? Why had he risked the loss of reputation and family for a fleeting thrill? As I analyzed the progression of mistakes that led to his fall, I discovered a method to the madness of immorality.

The Bible provides us with insights into the character of its heroes and heroines—warts and all. Noah drank to drunkenness, Abraham lied, Lot committed incest, and Moses killed a man. Later, Miriam and Aaron permitted their jealousy of Moses' privileged status to bring God's judgment. Because of Miriam's envy, God even afflicted her temporarily with leprosy.[1] The Bible doesn't hide the fact that many of the patriarchs, prophets, and saints had feet of clay.

As I studied these biblical examples, it was interesting to see how moral collapses have steps and stages. They may seem to happen suddenly and overnight, but insidious gradations exist that lead to ruin.

What is the method behind the madness of lust that makes us less safe in a dangerous world? In 2 Samuel 11, we see lust's *modus operandi* in destroying King David. Through shunned responsibility, excessive leisure, delayed resistance, self-importance, insufficient faith, callous conscience, and delayed recovery, David sent his life spinning out of control.

Handpicked by God to be King Saul's successor, David, who was called a man after God's own heart, is the last person we would expect to allow lust to steal his joy.[2] David possessed an exceptional passion for God—dancing and celebrating the return of the Ark of the Covenant in one famous instance.[3] Moreover, he authored lyrical poems to God, extolling the virtues of his Creator. And so sensitive was his conscience that he once expressed regret for cutting the garment of an enemy who sought to kill him.[4] Nevertheless, lust made David stumble and permanently tarnished his reputation.

FEARLESS PRINCIPLE: *Don't make excuses*

We sometimes blame our moral missteps on the uniqueness of the temptation.

"Nobody knows the trouble I've seen," intones an old Negro spiritual.

"This temptation seems unlike anything others have to endure," we say to ourselves.

This excuse is too flimsy to withstand scriptural scrutiny. The Bible assures us that the tests we face are common to humanity: "The temptations in your life are no different from what others experience."[5] Simply put, it means others are going through the same challenging experiences that you and I face.

In 1 Kings 19:14, the prophet Elijah complains to God: "The people of Israel have broken their covenant with you, torn down your altars, and killed every one of your prophets. I am the only one left, and now they are trying to kill me, too."

Later, God corrected the distorted thinking of this distraught prophet by saying, "I have reserved seven thousand in Israel, all whose knees have not bowed to Baal."[6] Elijah thought he was the only one in Israel who was seeking to faithfully serve God. He overlooked seven thousand others who should have been a source of encouragement to him.

A second excuse for moral lapses is that temptation overwhelms us. Again, 1 Corinthians 10:13 provides the rebuttal: "God is faithful. He will not allow the temptation to be more than you can stand. When you are tempted, he will show you a way out so that you can endure." In other words, God weighs the challenges we face and will only permit us to encounter what he knows we can handle. Great challenges serve to remind us that God is faithful and we may have underestimated our resources. Our greatest resource is the fact that God has promised to provide a way of escape for each temptation.

FEARLESS PRINCIPLE:
Don't shirk your responsibilities

How did David allow lust to lead him to failure in a dangerous world? He started by shirking his responsibilities. "In the spring, at the time when kings go off to war, David sent Joab out with the king's men and the whole Israelite army. . . . But David remained in Jerusalem."[7] As often happens, David succumbed to lust when he wasn't where he was supposed to be, doing what he was supposed to be doing.

In David's time, most soldiers were farmers, who often returned from the battle to plant their crops. Because it was springtime and the crops had already been planted, many of these citizen soldiers were free for combat. Routinely, they were led by the king but not this time. For some reason, David delegated this responsibility to Joab, his general. David shirked his duty.

What duties are you avoiding that could lead to a moral fall? Maybe you've forgotten who you are and what you're supposed to be doing:

> You are a chosen people. You are royal priests, a holy nation, God's very own possession. As a result, you can show others the goodness of God, for he called you out of the darkness into his wonderful light.[8]

In contrast to David, Bathsheba's husband, Uriah, had made a commitment to his military duty. He refuses to go home to the comfort of his wife as long as "the Ark and the armies of Israel and Judah are living in tents, and Joab and my master's men are camping in the open fields. . . . I swear that I would never do such a thing."[9] Uriah's fidelity to duty should have awakened in David a desire to return to the path of integrity, but it didn't. Lust overpowered reason.

FEARLESS PRINCIPLE: *Avoid excessive leisure*

Not only did David shirk his responsibilities, but he also permitted himself to be victimized by excessive leisure. "Late one afternoon, David got up from a nap and was walking around on the flat roof of his palace."[10] What's going on here? Why is the leader of a nation getting out of bed in the late afternoon? David not only delegated the job of leading his army into battle, but he was also lazing around at home.

During my college years, I sometimes felt embarrassed because I had to do manual labor. As one of the college custodians, I often watched the more privileged students driving around campus in their cars or walking with their sweethearts, while I picked up litter. They seemed to experience the joy of idleness, while I was forced to work.

I later discovered that my job was a blessing in disguise. For one thing, I never had a problem sleeping. I would fall asleep almost before my head touched the pillow. Moreover, several of the "fortunate ones" who didn't have to work were sent home midsemester. It seems their idleness gave way to some unethical acts. I began to feel better about my plight.

FEARLESS PRINCIPLE: *Don't procrastinate*

To defeat lust, we must not delay in resisting temptation. The story of Samson in Judges 16 provides a tragic example of a man who played with fire and was burned. Repeatedly, Delilah sought the secret of his strength. Toying with her, Samson acted as if he were playing a game. He kept giving Delilah bogus secrets to his strength even though it soon became obvious she meant to harm him. Repeatedly, Samson escaped her deceitful scheme and began to feel invincible. He delayed his resistance to temptation and lost his freedom, his sight, and eventually his life.

When confronted with evil, don't procrastinate. Resist early. Sin dies more quickly in its embryonic stage, so nip it in the bud.

FEARLESS PRINCIPLE: *Avoid self-importance*
David spotted a woman he fancied—Bathsheba—but when he learned she was the wife of one of his elite soldiers, it should have been sufficient to keep him from sin. Unfortunately, he permitted his privileged status to infuse him with a spirit of self-importance. After all, he was the king. Much like the rich man in the story the prophet Nathan later told him, David refused to deny himself, reasoning that his status made him the exception to the rule.

In my work on Capitol Hill, I meet people who are tempted by inflated feelings of self-importance. Typically, they are pursued by the press, courted by lobbyists, and celebrated by constituents. Countless stories can be told of politicians who allowed this favored treatment and exalted status to lead them into sin. Leaders often fall into transgression simply because they can, and the headlines reveal the details of their missteps. It's pure folly that permits feelings of self-importance to cloud their judgment and lead to a fall.

FEARLESS PRINCIPLE: *Exercise faith*
The Bible reminds us that whatever is not of faith is sin.[11] So much of sin's misery comes from not exercising our faith. When we fail to trust God to supply our needs and give us our heart's desires, we write a recipe for failure. In effect we're saying, "God, I'm smarter than you, so let me order my own steps." This shows a lack of faith and an arrogance that usually leads to ruin.

FEARLESS PRINCIPLE: *Don't sear your conscience*
When we make excuses, shirk our responsibilities, become lazy, procrastinate, give in to feelings of self-importance, and fail to exercise our faith, we risk searing our conscience, making it less sensitive

and less likely to safeguard us in dangerous times. For David, when Uriah demonstrated more integrity drunk than David did while sober, his conscience should have gone off like an alarm clock.[12] But David had neglected the call of conscience for so long that his conscience had become seared. Instead of feeling guilty and being led to repentance—like Peter after he had denied Jesus—David decided to kill Uriah, his faithful warrior. When we continually suppress or ignore the pangs of conscience, eventually we become desensitized to the very means by which the Holy Spirit often speaks to us. In David's case, it allowed one tragedy to grow into another of even greater magnitude.

FEARLESS PRINCIPLE: *Don't delay repentance*

After David failed to defeat lust and was led into deeper levels of sinful behavior, he made matters worse by engaging in a cover-up—sending Uriah to his death in battle (which cost the lives of several other soldiers, by the way) and taking Bathsheba as his wife.[13] For nearly a year, he sought to conceal what he had done. But delay only exacerbated the problem. Like the prodigal son in Luke 15, who continued in his transgressions until confronted with the truth of his situation while working in a pigpen in a far country, David kept up the charade until confronted with the truth of his situation by the prophet Nathan.[14] If only he had promptly repented . . .

Like David, why do we linger in our sin? Why are we so reluctant to confess and forsake our misdeeds? God promises that if we will "confess our sins to him, he is faithful and just to forgive us our sins and to cleanse us from all wickedness."[15]

The cancer of lust can keep us from thriving in a dangerous world, so let's avoid it by staying aware of the steps that can lead us to ruin. If we will exercise the following principles, we can defeat lust and live powerfully with abundant fulfillment, thriving in a wolf's world:

- Don't make excuses.
- Don't shirk your responsibilities.
- Avoid excessive leisure.
- Don't procrastinate.
- Avoid self-importance.
- Exercise faith.
- Don't sear your conscience.
- Don't delay repentance.

PURPOSEFUL PRAYER

Our Father, remind us that we will be judged by the fruit of our lives and that you require us to faithfully flee from the lust of the flesh. Make us good stewards of our talents and abilities so that our thoughts, words, and deeds will glorify your name. Inspire us to serve rather than be served, following your Son's example of humility and sacrifice. Open our minds to the unlimited possibilities available to those who trust you as their guide. We pray in Jesus' name. Amen.

LIVE WITHOUT SLOTH

THOMAS EDISON, explaining his success as an inventor, once said, "Genius is one percent inspiration, 99 percent perspiration."[1] Edison's words are a fitting rebuke to the slothful and lazy and a very appropriate statement from a man of diligence, who made several thousand attempts before successfully inventing the incandescent lightbulb.

Many fail to discover their destiny because of laziness and idleness. Thousands are harmed each day because of sloth. It brings poverty, bondage, conceit, scarcity, and folly.

The downward slope of sloth
Laziness has been the bane of human existence for as long as there has been work to avoid. In *The Prophet*, Kahlil Gibran suggests that idlers are out of step with nature: "You work that you may keep pace with the earth and the soul of the earth, for to be idle is to become

a stranger unto the seasons, and to step out of life's procession that marches in majesty and proud submission towards the infinite."[2]

Some time ago, I visited Lexington Market in Baltimore, where I grew up. I entered this historic place of pleasant foods and culinary delights and noticed that many immigrants were selling the distinctive cuisines of their homelands. Sadly, I found not a single establishment representing my ethnic group, and I pondered the possible reasons. Not ignoring racism's realities, I concluded that the absence of a vigorous work ethic is often the reason why many fail to maximize their possibilities. Diligence is needed for success in nearly every endeavor. As it says in Proverbs, "All hard work brings a profit, but mere talk leads only to poverty."[3]

Poverty

Poverty is one consequence of indolence. Sloth also causes apathy. According to Proverbs 12:27, "Lazy people don't even cook the game they catch." We see a similar sentiment in Proverbs 26:15: "Lazy people take food in their hand but don't even lift it to their mouth." Many people never achieve their potential because of the apathy that accompanies their habitual laziness.

When I occasionally visit the old inner-city neighborhoods where I grew up, inevitably I see people standing on the street corners, milling around and wasting valuable time. "What's going on?" I inquire. "What's happening?"

"Nothing much" is the usual response.

"Why aren't you guys working?"

"I can't find a job," many will say. Some, it seems, blame "the man"—by this they mean ubiquitous discrimination—for making them accept their depressing situation. "The man just won't give me a break."

This unfortunate apathy often leads to waste. "He who is slothful in his work is a brother to him who is a great destroyer."[4] Jesus says something similar in Luke 10:2: "The harvest is great, but the workers are few." Many crops will never be harvested because of the indolence of people who are unwilling to work. Many talents and abilities are never developed because of laziness. This deprives society of desperately needed services, inventions, and fresh opportunities. Imagine if Beethoven had decided never to play the piano or Michelangelo refused to ever pick up a paintbrush or Jesus decided not to enter public ministry.

The United Negro College Fund's slogan is "A mind is a terrible thing to waste." This nonprofit organization seeks to motivate people to contribute money so that underprivileged students can receive an education. If people cannot find meaningful work, they often do nothing—which only contributes to the tragic waste of talent and genius in our society and world.

Bondage

Many addictions come about because people have too little to do. Often we read about wealthy young people who develop addictions because they have too much time on their hands. Some develop friendships with alcohol, drugs, pornography, and promiscuity because they fritter away their time on trivialities. They party with their friends and develop debilitating habits that eventually mortgage their future.

Many years ago, I began playing chess. At first, I lost nearly every game. But then I bought some books about chess and began to study, practice, and get better at the intricacies of the game. As I started winning, the game became addicting. All of my spare time was spent playing. I would fly to New York from DC on the weekends to participate in chess matches and feed my desire for the game. On more than one occasion, my wife asked me, "Honey, don't you think you've purchased enough chess books?"

One time when she asked about my books, I proceeded to my library to count them. After tallying more than a hundred, I concluded the time had come to be released from this addiction. So I let it go. Too much valuable time had evaporated before my eyes with this trivial pursuit.

Conceit

Sloth also leads to conceit. "The lazy man is wiser in his own eyes than seven men who can answer sensibly."[5] In other words, without taking time to do their homework, idlers ignore the wisdom of many advisors. They accept as sufficient their superficial analysis of the difficulties they face. They feel that further study is unnecessary, something that merely wearies the flesh.

In the Oscar-winning movie *Rocky*, heavyweight champion Apollo Creed believes that challenger Rocky Balboa is a pushover, thus any serious preparation for their upcoming title bout is unnecessary. When Creed's advisors become alarmed at his indifferent fight preparation, he is unmoved. He eventually loses his championship because of laziness and conceit.

Scarcity

Sloth also brings scarcity. An old adage declares, "When we sleep during harvest time, the crops rot on the vine." If we allow sloth to keep us from our anointed purpose, the profit we might otherwise receive will disappear, and lack will become the norm. Proverbs 10:4 says, "A slack hand becomes poor."[6] A willingness to work can mean the difference between making it and losing out because "in all labor there is profit."[7]

After my middle son graduated from Yale University, I asked him, "What really is the difference between an Ivy League education and a less prestigious one?" As a transfer student to Yale, he gave this perspective: "Dad, it's the work ethic. It's not that Ivy League students are so much smarter. Yes, many are bright, but, oh, how they work, studying sometimes for thirty-six consecutive hours for one exam.

At my other school, many of the students I knew allowed laziness to lead to missed opportunities." Sloth often brings scarcity.

Folly

Sloth often contributes to folly. One day I asked a college professor friend, "What has surprised you the most in your twenty-five years of teaching?"

He thoughtfully responded, "Young people who come from excellent homes and are financially secure often do stupid things and fall far below the expected standard. This startles me. I'm also surprised by students who come from privation but flourish nonetheless." Indeed the well-off who embrace folly often are victims of idleness and sloth, lending truth to the maxim "An idle mind is the devil's workshop."

So what can we do to avoid the slippery slope of sloth?

FEARLESS PRINCIPLE: *Don't waste opportunities*

To succeed against sloth, we must seize opportunities. One of my friends is a novelist who regularly turns out new books. One time I asked her, "How do you manage such a great literary output?"

"Barry," she said. "I'm surprised you would ask that question. I simply strive to write one page each day. That's at least a book a year." She manages her time so that, page by page, she moves toward her goal. That is making the most of every day and seizing the opportunity. *Carpe diem.*

One way to avoid wasting opportunities is to be unafraid of doing something poorly. Better or best is often the enemy of good enough. Perfectionism can lead to the paralysis of analysis. As Ecclesiastes 11:4 puts it, "Farmers who wait for perfect weather never plant. If they watch every cloud, they never harvest."

Don't be victimized by the temptation to wait for perfect circumstances. The ad writers for Nike captured an essential truth when they came up with the classic tagline "Just do it."

FEARLESS PRINCIPLE: *Don't love slumber*

To succeed against sloth, we must resist the love of slumber. In Romans 13:11-12, Paul tells us, "It is high time to awake out of sleep; for now our salvation is nearer than when we first believed. The night is far spent, the day is at hand. Therefore let us cast off the works of darkness, and let us put on the armor of light."[8]

In college, my love of slumber caused me to use the snooze button far too often. It reached a point where I could press the button while continuing to sleep. One fateful morning, I had a Greek exam scheduled for 8:00 a.m. After studying assiduously into the early morning hours, I finally set my alarm and went to bed, anticipating an early morning departure. When I awakened, the sun was already high in the sky. I knew in an instant, "Houston, we have a problem." It was too bright to be 7:00 a.m.; and in fact it was noon. My desire for sleep resulted in a missed examination and a less than exemplary final grade.

FEARLESS PRINCIPLE: *Develop your capacity*

To succeed against sloth, we must develop our capacity. This means weeding out distractions and building up productive resources. The book of Proverbs illustrates this principle with the example of a vineyard:

> I walked by the field of a lazy person, the vineyard of one with
> no common sense. I saw that it was overgrown with nettles.
> It was covered with weeds, and its walls were broken down.
> Then, as I looked and thought about it, I learned this lesson:
> A little extra sleep, a little more slumber, a little folding of the
> hands to rest—then poverty will pounce on you like a bandit;
> scarcity will attack you like an armed robber.[9]

Avoiding sloth and developing our capacity require diligence, perseverance, and wisdom. If we allow our lives to be overgrown with nettles and weeds and our walls to crumble from neglect, we will fail to develop the capacity that God desires for our lives.

Developing our capacity is an ongoing and gradual process. I once had lunch with Steven Covey, the well-known and successful author of several significant self-help books. During the meal, he said, "You can't cram on a farm." In other words, we can't wait until just before the harvest to plant our seeds. We must capitalize on the progression of seasons—cultivating, sowing, pruning, and reaping all in due course. Sowing and reaping take time, and they must be done in the proper season. Likewise, developing our capacity for whatever God has in store for our lives is a time-consuming, progressive, seasonal process. Just as we can't cram on a farm, we can't cram in our spiritual lives either.

In Matthew 25, the parable of the talents demonstrates the importance of developing our capacity. Only those who invested wisely reaped a return. The man who refused to develop his gift, who buried it in the earth, received a rebuke from his master. In the end, his one bag of silver was taken from him and given to others. God expects us to develop and utilize our capacity.

FEARLESS PRINCIPLE: *Don't neglect spiritual exercise*

To succeed against sloth, we mustn't neglect spiritual exercise. Spiritual sloth can be as injurious as physical laziness. When we neglect our spiritual fitness and are too lazy to nourish our souls, we pave the way for ethical malnutrition. Then, when temptations come and we need a robust spiritual strength to overcome them, our spiritual immune system will be too weak.

On the night when he was betrayed, Jesus exercised spiritual diligence, praying for hours in the garden of Gethsemane.[10] Meanwhile, his hand-selected companions—Peter, James, and John—dozed off. These disciples, particularly Peter, soon found themselves ill prepared for the challenges that tested their spiritual readiness. Are you too busy to take time to develop your spiritual stamina? Will neglect of spiritual exercise make you a candidate for succumbing to sin?

FEARLESS PRINCIPLE: *Don't live on good intentions*

To succeed against sloth, we must go beyond mere good intentions. I'm sure the lazy person depicted in Proverbs 24:30-34 fully intended to do his work. He simply needed a little nap first. But good intentions seldom get the job done; they must be accompanied by purposeful action. The five foolish bridesmaids in Matthew 25 fully intended to be prepared for the arrival of the bridegroom. But they weren't. When he came unexpectedly while they were off replenishing their depleted oil supply, all their good intentions couldn't save them from great disappointment.

FEARLESS PRINCIPLE: *Live for God's glory*

To succeed against sloth, we must live for God's glory, not our own satisfaction or fulfillment. We're challenged in 1 Corinthians 10:31 to do everything for God's glory, whether we're eating or drinking or playing. This is the highest calling for humanity—not family, or country, or race, or ambition, or happiness. God's glory must be our paramount aim. Living for God's glory should affect our choice of employment, our choice of friends, our choice of where to live, and our choice of life direction. Laboring to please God alone is a sure way to succeed against sloth.

———————

We all can succeed against sloth and reach our potential for excellence. To overcome laziness and thrive in a threatening world, remember these principles:

- Don't waste opportunities.
- Don't love slumber.

- Develop your capacity.
- Don't neglect spiritual exercise.
- Don't live on good intentions.
- Live for God's glory.

PURPOSEFUL PRAYER

Holy Spirit, save us from sloth and give us a social conscience built on the vision of the ancient prophets, who saw sufficiency for every person. Use us to hasten the day when the small and weak can make their contributions alongside the great and powerful. Lead us on a path that will empower us to foster peace on earth, when swords shall be beaten into plowshares and humanity will study war no more. Help us to remember that the hands of the diligent will rule. We pray in the awesome name of Jesus. Amen.

LIVE WITHOUT DESTRUCTIVE ANGER

DID JESUS EVER BECOME ANGRY? Mark 3:1-6 tells the story of a time when Jesus healed a man on the Sabbath while the religious leaders stood in judgment of him. Mark reports that Jesus "looked around at them angrily and was deeply saddened by their hard hearts."[1] We can be certain that if Jesus became angry, his indignation was commingled with grief, and he constructively managed his wrath. If the Messiah, our divine role model, expressed appropriate anger, you and I can become angry without falling into sin. Though anger can often be a destructive force, appropriate anger can be expressed constructively.

During my freshman year in college, my fellow students launched a cafeteria strike. Student leaders made the announcement: "As a protest against the inferior food, no student should eat in the cafeteria." I worked on campus as a janitor. As the dinner hour approached, I found myself gripped with anger—at the protesting students, not the cafeteria. Many of these students didn't have to work to pay their tuition, but I did. Some came from homes where palatable and well-balanced meals were the norm, but I didn't. Growing up on welfare, I sometimes had no food at all. With that in mind, I decided to challenge the strike. After all, the cafeteria food was considerably better than the meals I ate at home. Suddenly, my indignation motivated me to buck peer pressure and cross the picket line.

"Traitor!" someone shouted.

"There's always one who won't play with the team," taunted another.

Then I heard the pleading voice of my girlfriend: "Barry, please don't do this to me."

Undeterred, I put one foot in front of the other until I came to a greatly desired plate of food and sat down. One other student joined me in this lonely counterprotest, and we both reaped the disdain of the nearly nine hundred students who voluntarily fasted. In retrospect, I made the right decision, and it demonstrates how anger can be used constructively.

Unfortunately, anger is all too often destructive, causing us to behave foolishly.

In Genesis 4, we read about how destructive anger motivated Cain to kill his brother, Abel. Destructive anger caused Joseph's brothers to nurture homicidal thoughts and sell him into Egyptian slavery.[2] Destructive anger prompted Pharaoh to force the Israelite slaves to gather their own straw to make bricks.[3] Destructive anger was at the root of Eliab's criticism of David in 1 Samuel 17. And destructive anger fueled Nebuchadnezzar's order to heat the fiery furnace with greater intensity before tossing in Shadrach, Meshach, and Abednego.[4]

In the aftermath of destructive anger, wars are fought, homes are ruined, and nations are tossed onto history's scrap heap. Destructive anger contributes to the quiet desperation that thousands experience as they fail to thrive fearlessly in a dangerous world.

In the book of Jonah, we read about a prophet's anger that almost had destructive consequences.

> Jonah was really upset and angry. So he prayed:
>
> Our LORD, I knew from the very beginning that you wouldn't destroy Nineveh. That's why I left my own country and headed for Spain. You are a kind and merciful God, and you are very patient. You always show love, and you don't like to punish anyone, not even foreigners.
>
> Now let me die! I'd be better off dead.
>
> The LORD replied, "What right do you have to be angry?"[5]

Jonah had been commissioned by God to preach to the wicked inhabitants of the city of Nineveh. His message was simple but disturbing: "Forty days from now, Nineveh will be destroyed!"[6]

The people of Nineveh didn't react as Jonah expected. Instead of ignoring his sermon, they repented and turned to God—from the king on his throne down to the peasants working in the fields. Even the animals were forced to fast. When God saw how Nineveh's people had been transformed by Jonah's preaching, he didn't destroy the city. This infuriated Jonah, who despised the Ninevites.

God decided to teach Jonah a lesson about anger:

> The LORD made a vine grow up to shade Jonah's head and protect him from the sun. Jonah was very happy to have the vine, but early the next morning the LORD sent a worm to chew on the vine, and the vine dried up. During the day the LORD sent a scorching wind, and the sun beat down on Jonah's head, making him feel faint. Jonah was ready to die, and he shouted, "I wish I were dead!"
>
> But the LORD asked, "Jonah, do you have the right to be angry about the vine?"

"Yes, I do," he answered, "and I'm angry enough to die."

But the LORD said:

You are concerned about a vine that you did not plant or take care of, a vine that grew up in one night and died the next. In that city of Nineveh there are more than a hundred twenty thousand people who cannot tell right from wrong, and many cattle are also there. Don't you think I should be concerned about that big city?[7]

How can we learn to live without the destructive consequences of anger?

FEARLESS PRINCIPLE: *Develop compassion*

God used Jonah's anger to develop compassion in him. Jonah's corrupted sense of privilege prompted him to feel more regret over the loss of a plant than the potential destruction of tens of thousands of people. How often do we become angry over the misery we see in the world—compared to how often we get mad about comparatively trivial things?

Nearly every day, I pass through Union Station near the US Capitol in Washington, DC. Strewn about the area are the human debris of our nation—the hungry, the homeless, and the hopeless. As I see people sleeping on newspapers or begging for food, I feel angry. How can we in this prosperous country permit such pathology to exist in the shadow of our great monuments? Appropriately managed anger can engender compassion.

In Matthew 25, Jesus tells the story of Judgment Day.[8] Humanity's masses are divided into two groups: sheep and goats. Each group is judged, and the criteria are the same. Did you feed the hungry, clothe the naked, and visit the sick and incarcerated? Jesus says that when we exhibit compassion for "the least of these," we demonstrate compassion to him. Why not find joy in letting anger disturb your spirit into compassionate action? Although as individuals we cannot completely repair the hurts of our world, we can make a dent in the misery. And when we do, we serve Christ with love.

FEARLESS PRINCIPLE: *Seek redemption, not revenge*

God also helped Jonah see the redemptive power of well-managed anger. God is in the business of saving people—redeeming the lost. Jonah's anger made him prefer destruction over salvation.

Most Americans are aware of how the organization Mothers Against Drunk Driving (MADD) began. Its origins demonstrate the appropriate channeling of anger. After losing a daughter to the idiocy of an inebriated driver, one mother decided to use her anger constructively. She started MADD, a life-saving organization that has helped our society become less tolerant of those who drink and drive. Anger can save lives.

FEARLESS PRINCIPLE: *Constructively manage your anger*

Anger can be constructively managed—especially when it is proportional, unselfish, impersonal, and brief. As Paul advises, "Don't get so angry that you sin. Don't go to bed angry and don't give the devil a chance."[9]

How can we incorporate these principles into our quest for joyful living? First, harness anger by keeping it proportional. This simply means that we scale our wrath to fit the offense. We don't execute people for misdemeanors. When King Saul became angry with his son Jonathan for being David's friend, he threw a spear in an attempt to kill him.[10] Fortunately, the spear missed Jonathan, but Saul was venting his disproportionate anger in a foolish and nearly tragic way.

Like Saul, we can permit excessive anger to steal our joy. Most of us remember the story of the Hatfields and the McCoys, two families who famously feuded. Ignited by excessive anger, their animosity continued for many years—so long, in fact, that the families couldn't remember what had started it. Constructively managed anger is proportional to the offense.

Next, we can harness our anger with unselfishness. Have you ever noticed that Jesus only became angry in defense of others, never on his own behalf? Even when they crucified him, he never expressed anger—only unselfish compassion. But when the religious leaders exploited the people by charging inflated prices in the Temple, Jesus called them thieves and started knocking over tables in anger.[11] Appropriate anger is altruistic and selfless, and it takes decisive action when appropriate.

We can also harness anger by staying objective. One maxim declares, "Love the sinner, but hate the evil deed." We should not direct our anger at people, but at changing the injustice and remedying the problem. President Abraham Lincoln was a champion of objective and effective action. He channeled his anger into efforts to eliminate slavery but didn't act in malice against the slave owners.

Finally, we can harness our anger by keeping it brief. "Don't let the sun go down while you are still angry."[12] This brief anger is beautifully modeled by God himself: "For his anger lasts only a moment, but his favor lasts a lifetime! Weeping may last through the night, but joy comes with the morning."[13]

As we learn to thrive fearlessly in a threatening world, we can harness the energy of constructive anger—keeping it proportional, unselfish, impersonal, and brief—by observing these guidelines:

- Develop compassion.
- Seek redemption, not revenge.
- Constructively manage your anger.

PURPOSEFUL PRAYER

Our Father, let your glory cover all the earth. Teach us to harness our anger and sin not. Strengthen us for life's challenges. We need your grace, for we cannot offer anything to merit your favor or gain your love. Empower us to travel today's journey in a way that will receive your divine approval. Give us confidence to draw near to you that we may find grace to help us in our time of need. We trust in your powerful name. Amen.

LIVE WITHOUT GREED

"I'M SORRY, CHAPLAIN, but I'm not in the mood for a Bible study today."

These words surprised me because they were uttered by one of our more faithful legislative leaders. I sympathized with him in his pain, but there seemed little I could do to help him. He had lost nearly everything he owned during the ravaging one-two punch of Hurricanes Katrina and Rita, and no easy theological rhetoric could assuage his pain.

Two weeks sped by, and I saw him at another Bible study. "I missed you at our last two studies," I said.

"I'm sorry, Chaplain. I've been busy, but I'm all right now."

"I don't want to open old wounds," I responded, "but you seem to be on top of things now. What's going on?"

"Chaplain," he said, "it's truly amazing. We rear our children, and if we're fortunate, we may live long enough for them to rear us."

"That sounds clever," I said. "What does it mean?"

"I'm thinking about my daughter," he said with a smile. "God used her to help me stop feeling sorry for myself."

"I'd like to hear about that. What happened?"

"Well, while visiting my daughter and feeling sorry for myself, I began complaining about my losses. No one seemed to be able to say anything to give me a more positive perspective on my setbacks, but suddenly my daughter opened my eyes. She interrupted my litany of negativity with these simple words: 'Oh, Daddy, it's just stuff.' Don't ask me why, Chaplain, but those three words, *It's just stuff*, changed my perspective, and I found myself chuckling. She's right, you know. All of it—it's just stuff."

Greed involves a preoccupation with stuff. It is an excessive desire to acquire or possess more than one needs or deserves, and it can wreak havoc on contentment and joyful living.

Greed cast a shadow on the lives of such biblical characters as Balaam, Achan, Gehazi, and Judas. Its potential as a pitfall is captured in the words of Ecclesiastes 4:6: "Yet a very little food eaten in peace is better than twice as much earned from overwork and chasing the wind."[1] Greed can make us dissatisfied with the bird we have in hand so that we lose our peace in quest of the elusive bird in the bush.

To thrive fearlessly in a dangerous world, we must avoid greed and see it from a proper perspective. Jesus once observed that "one's life does not consist in the abundance of his possessions."[2] He says something similar in Matthew 4:4: "Man shall not live by bread alone, but by every word that comes from the mouth of God."[3] Jesus highlights the efficacy of spiritual things to satisfy us in ways that mere *stuff* cannot.

FEARLESS PRINCIPLE:
Be satisfied with the bare necessities
Why do material resources fail to satisfy our deepest needs? First, very little is actually needed for a fulfilling existence. As Paul suggested

to his young protégé Timothy: "If we have food and clothing, with these we will be content."[4]

I like to play a game with the Senate pages—the high school students who work on Capitol Hill. During roll call votes when most of the senators are present, I challenge the pages: "Look at the way our senators are dressed and tell me which ones are millionaires." Although approximately half of our senators are millionaires, the pages are unable to discern the truly wealthy from the others. After a while, all the black, blue, gray, and tan suits begin to look the same, and 100 percent wool looks pretty good, whether it's tailor-made or purchased off the rack. I use that teachable moment to point out the limitations of wealth.

Occasionally, when seated in the Senate dining room, I'll notice very wealthy legislators eating the same food as the rest of us. They may be worth tens of millions of dollars, but nothing they can purchase in the dining room is beyond the reach of my wallet. When we learn to be content with what we have, we may find that what we have is quite satisfying and sufficient. But when our eyes tempt us to become greedy, we can fall into a world of hurt. Consider the cautionary example of Elisha's servant Gehazi.

We meet Gehazi in 2 Kings 5, just after Elisha has healed Naaman, the Syrian general, of leprosy. Elisha refuses remuneration for this miracle, which displeases Gehazi, who sees no harm in accepting a few gifts from the grateful general. "My master doesn't know what's best for him," he muses. Consumed by greed, he embarks on a plan to reclaim the profit his master has refused.

Gehazi pursues Naaman and concocts a lie. "Two young prophets have just arrived to visit my master," he says. "So my master would like the money you offered and a few garments to help them."[5]

Naaman is more than happy to oblige, sending servants to help carry Gehazi's new wealth back to his home. When he arrives at home, Gehazi hides his spoils.

Eventually, Elisha sends for his servant. "Where have you been, Gehazi?"

"I haven't been anywhere," he replied.

Elisha said, "Did my heart not go out with you when the general gave you those gifts? Now, Naaman's leprosy will be upon you and your descendants forever."

When Gehazi left the presence of Elisha, he was covered with leprosy, his skin as white as snow.[6]

FEARLESS PRINCIPLE:
Don't presume upon religious advantage

Gehazi's story teaches us some valuable lessons about dealing with greed. First, if we are to live without greed, we must never take our standing before God for granted. As the apostle Paul says, "Shall we go on sinning so that grace may increase? By no means! We are those who have died to sin; how can we live in it any longer?"[7] One would think that Gehazi, as a servant of the most prominent prophet of his time, would have a pretty firm handle on right and wrong. Yet he decides to deviate from the path of strict integrity.

It was as if he said, "Why shouldn't I get some benefit from my association with Elisha?"

Ongoing exposure to the spiritual advantages of our relationship with God can often desensitize us to compromise and sin. As we become accustomed to following Jesus, we may lose our sense of wonder, allowing familiarity to breed contempt. Sacred music, which once lifted our spirits, can become passé. Powerful biblical passages that once strengthened our faith can begin to seem trite. Such desensitization may be the prelude to a lax attitude about our walk with Jesus, prompting some of us to take for granted what should be held sacred.

This attitude is particularly prevalent among the children of spiritual leaders, who often grow up feeling as if God is a grandparent and they have a special "insider" status when it comes to getting prayers answered and receiving divine favor. As a preacher and the father of three sons, I've seen this phenomenon up close and personal. My boys grew up surrounded by religious symbols and jargon. They spent more time at church than most of their friends. I encouraged them to remember that God has no grandchildren, only sons and daughters, and that they must develop their own relationship with him. Like the sons of Aaron or Eli, those reared in preachers' homes may become too casual and even negligent about holy things.[8]

FEARLESS PRINCIPLE: *Avoid covetousness*

Putting off greed means that we must avoid covetousness, which steals our joy by impelling us to desire something that someone else possesses. Just as King Ahab desired Naboth's vineyard in 1 Kings 21, we pine for the car, home, or spouse of our neighbor, a practice expressly forbidden by the tenth commandment.[9]

Gehazi gave in to covetousness. He saw his master missing an opportunity for gain, and he desired the offered gifts for himself. Covetousness drove him to lie and deceive, actions that cost him a painful price when his sin came to light.

It's important to keep covetousness in proper perspective. It is the first cousin of greed, and too many people lose the joy of one full hand by desiring to see their second hand full as well. Nevertheless, covetousness can actually be a positive thing when it compels us to pursue the best. As 1 Corinthians 12:31 puts it, we should "earnestly desire the best gifts."[10]

How easy it is for us to be quite satisfied with what we have until we see something that a neighbor owns. You were quite happy with your old car until you saw your next-door neighbor drive home in a shiny new toy. Your home was pleasant and comfortable until you attended a friend's Christmas party and saw what they had done to their place.

A good way to counteract greed is to learn to "rejoice with those who rejoice."[11] Learn to celebrate the good fortune of others, knowing that your season for a productive harvest cannot be stopped. Genesis 8:22 reminds us that seedtime and harvest will continue "as long as the earth remains." Our harvest is as certain as the coming of morning, for we reap what we sow.[12]

FEARLESS PRINCIPLE: *Flee lies and deceptions*

Gehazi lied and deceived to achieve his nefarious ends. Proverbs 12:22 reminds us, "Lying lips are an abomination to the Lord, but those who act faithfully are his delight."[13] Lies and deception steal our joy. I learned this at the age of five. While eating from the peanut butter jar one day with my fingers instead of using a utensil, I heard the ominous sound of my mother's footsteps approaching. Knowing that judgment was near, I hid the peanut butter jar and prepared to deceive Mama. I sighed with relief when she appeared and seemed unaware of my misbehavior . . . until she spoke.

"Are you all right, son?"

"Yes, ma'am," I responded cautiously.

"Barry, have you been in the peanut butter?"

That question put me in a quandary. How could she possibly know? I began an internal cost/benefits analysis. What's the probability that I can lie and escape this predicament? I gambled.

"No, ma'am, I haven't been eating the peanut butter." My voice was calm, my gaze unwavering. No one had taught me to lie. I wouldn't have been able to define it for anyone, yet intuitively I sensed what needed to be done to successfully deceive. My ruse failed.

Leaving the kitchen, my mother returned with a mirror. Handing it to me, she said, "Look at your face."

Grasping the mirror with nervous hands, I glanced at my peanut–butter-covered face. The incriminating evidence shouted my guilt.

FEARLESS PRINCIPLE: *Cut your losses*

If Gehazi had not lied to Elisha and instead cut his losses, he may have escaped the bitter penalty of permanent leprosy, not only for himself but also for his descendants. Apparently, greed was too strong a motivation, and he gambled his life in an effort to hang on to his ill-gotten wealth.

In the parable of the Prodigal Son, I have often wondered why the younger son didn't simply cut his losses and return home shortly after leaving. He showed an arrogant disregard for his father's authority by leaving home in the first place. Then he wasted his money on wild living in a distant land, and still he did not repent when his friends and resources vanished. He remained stubborn as a great famine swept through the land, and still he wouldn't go home, instead accepting a job feeding pigs, a great humiliation for a Jewish lad. He returned home only after sinking to an all-time low, but what he found when he arrived was a father waiting with abundant forgiveness. Once he decided to cut his losses and return home, the prodigal son was able to see all that he had to gain.

We can put away our greed and learn to thrive fearlessly in a threatening world by investing in heaven's treasures and by following these guidelines for success:

- Be satisfied with the bare necessities.
- Don't presume upon religious advantage.
- Avoid covetousness.
- Flee lies and deceptions.
- Cut your losses.

PURPOSEFUL PRAYER

Immortal God, we acknowledge your power, mercy, and grace. Deliver us from greed, reminding us that our lives don't consist of the abundance of our possessions. May we pass this day in the companionship of your everlasting mercy, making time to be still and commune with you. Give us the wisdom to be responsible stewards of our time, energy, and abundance. In our decision making, guide us with the unfolding of your prevailing providence. Remind us that we can accomplish great things with cooperation but achieve little with criticism, selfishness, and greed. We praise your name. Amen.

LIVE WITHOUT GLUTTONY

WHEN I RETIRED FROM THE MILITARY, my physician gave me an exit examination. But now it had been six months since my last physical, and my new doctor expressed concern.

"What have you been doing?"

His question puzzled me.

"Is everything all right, Doc? What seems to be the problem?" I asked with urgency.

"Your physical condition has deteriorated dramatically in six months," he said. "What have you been doing?"

As I prepared to answer him, I thought about my recent lapses of far too much food and too little exercise. Tantalized by fancy restaurants in faraway places, I had been overeating, consuming too much of a good thing. Excessive indulgence had negatively affected my blood pressure, cholesterol levels, and other vital bodily functions. I proceeded to confess the extent of my intemperance to my concerned physician.

Gluttony brings negative consequences, and thriving in a threatening world requires that we starve this tendency.

Gluttony is more prevalent in our modern world than we sometimes realize. Current euphemisms for gluttony include *full-figured, plus size, big boned, heavyset, large, XXL, overweight,* and *out of shape.* The problem of gluttony can be seen in the billions of dollars spent each year by people trying to overcome it through dieting and fitness efforts. The pitfall of gluttony is alive and well in our time.

Gluttony keeps us from holy living. Engaging in excess of any kind is inconsistent with the requirements of spiritual fitness. As the apostle Peter says, "You have had enough in the past of the evil things that godless people enjoy—their immorality and lust, their feasting and drunkenness and wild parties, and their terrible worship of idols."[1] This verse speaks about the excesses that often accompany gluttony, making it clear that those who seek to glorify God will not engage in such behavior.

Are you attempting to maintain consistency in your spiritual walk? By putting off gluttony, you will honor God and reveal his power to unbelievers. As you learn to say no to fleshly impulses and gain the upper hand on the desire for immediate gratification, others will see your restraint and glorify God.

Proverbs 23:20-21 reminds us that gluttony often leads to poverty: "Do not carouse with drunkards or feast with gluttons, for they are on their way to poverty."

Failure to starve gluttony can lead to emotional distress as we continually pursue more, more, more. But as Ecclesiastes tells us, "Better one handful with tranquility than two handfuls with toil and chasing after the wind."[2]

Gluttony—which can be seen as a compulsive dissatisfaction with what we have—leads us far too often to complicate our lives to the point of despair. Voraciously, we attempt to keep up with the Joneses and stay ahead of the Smiths, only to discover that we're chasing illusions.

Gluttony can cause us to devalue spiritual things. Esau famously made this mistake when he traded his birthright for a pot of lentil stew.[3]

What kind of example does your eating set? When people see you eat, is it glorifying to God? The Bible says that it should be. "Whether you eat or drink, or whatever you do, do it all for the glory of God."[4] Those who watch us eat can be challenged to exercise greater self-discipline if we show the appropriate restraint.

When I was a young chaplain, I was invited to dine with one of our senior leaders. I piled my plate with wonderful food, as if I would never eat again. When my dining companion came to the table with a simple salad, I felt embarrassed. I learned that day that less is sometimes more. Later that afternoon, I fought to keep from dozing off as a result of my excessive eating.

FEARLESS PRINCIPLE: *Fight gluttony*

To fight gluttony, we must first value the spiritual over the physical. People do not "live by bread alone, but by every word that comes from the mouth of God."[5] Focusing on the spiritual is important because "the things we see now will soon be gone, but the things we cannot see will last forever."[6]

Second, we must develop the discipline of self-control. The apostle Paul refers to this when he declares, "Every athlete exercises self-control. . . . I discipline my body and keep it under control, lest after preaching to others I myself should be disqualified."[7] And indeed, self-control is evidence of the Holy Spirit's fruitful work in our lives.[8]

Finally, we must trust God to supply our needs "from his glorious riches."[9] Often, gluttony and excess come from our fear that we'll lack something in the future. When we acknowledge that our sovereign God has promised to supply our needs from his own vast resources, it frees us from the need to hoard or overindulge.

To thrive in a dangerous world, we must fight gluttony, realize that what we've been given is sufficient, and understand that less is often more.

PURPOSEFUL PRAYER

Eternal God, help us to live in a manner that the generations to come will know of your mighty acts. Give us the singularity of heart to see, find, and follow your will so that our legacy will be exemplary. Guide us today in the path you have created, inspiring us with the potency of your powerful presence. Save us from gluttony as we remember that our bodies are temples of your Holy Spirit. We praise your name. Amen.

LIVE WITHOUT ENVY

MY NEIGHBOR PULLED into the driveway in a shiny Mercedes.

"Is that your new car?" I asked.

"Yes," he responded. "And it drives like a dream. Would you like to take a spin?"

"I'm busy now, but I'll take a rain check," I responded with as much enthusiasm as I could muster. Entering my garage and looking at my twelve-year-old vehicle, I felt a sudden twinge of envy. My reliable transportation now seemed seriously deficient. I found myself feeling envious.

Do you sometimes find yourself wishing for something you don't have?

Growing up, I memorized a quote from George Bernard Shaw's play *Man and Superman*: "There are two tragedies in life. One is to lose your heart's desire. The other is to gain it." This is another way of suggesting we should be careful what we wish for, for we just might get it.

When we do get what we think we want, we often realize the foolishness of envy—which might be well defined as sadness in response to another's success. Envy rears its ugly head throughout the Bible. Cain became envious when God accepted his brother Abel's sacrifice and rejected his offering.[1] Rachel was envious of Leah, who was able to bear children for Jacob when she could not.[2] But at the same time, Leah was envious of Rachel, who was clearly Jacob's favorite.[3] Moses was envied by his siblings, Aaron and Miriam, and Daniel's enemies were envious enough to want to murder him.[4] Even Jesus had to deal with others' envy, as the priests who hated his success conspired to kill him.[5] If Jesus had to deal with being envied, certainly we will too as his followers.

Envy, which rides on the wings of hostility and ill will, is closely linked to jealousy and rivalry. It grows from a bitter root that desires to deprive others of what they have. We see this clearly in the life of Joseph, who was the object of fierce envy from his older brothers.[6] Joseph survived to discover his destiny and to go from adequacy to abundance, becoming Egypt's prime minister.[7] In the course of his lifetime, Joseph learned to sidestep envy and thrive in spite of external circumstances. How can we learn to do the same?

FEARLESS PRINCIPLE:
Expect trouble from unlikely sources

The darts of envy can come from unlikely sources. Jesus said, "A person's enemies will be those of his own household."[8] When David asked questions about fighting Goliath, his brother Eliab opposed him, speaking in words dripping with envy: "What are you doing here, anyway? Who's taking care of that little flock of sheep out in the desert? You spoiled brat! You came here just to watch the fighting, didn't you?"[9] As the eldest brother, Eliab should have been the last source of David's opposition. Instead, he was the first.

Jesus encountered similar opposition. The priests and religious leaders who envied him helped to orchestrate his crucifixion.[10] This was an unlikely source. The people who should have celebrated his good works saw him as a threat to the religious status quo, and they arranged for one of his own disciples, Judas, to betray him with a kiss. Those who would avoid envy must be prepared for unexpected attacks from unlikely sources. So how can we sidestep the temptation to want what others have or resent their success?

FEARLESS PRINCIPLE: *Develop a vigorous work ethic*

Joseph sidestepped his brothers' envy with a vigorous work ethic. Though they sold him into slavery, he labored with such diligence wherever he found himself, blooming where he was planted, that he became an indispensable leader. He worked with diligence and integrity in the home of Potiphar and became a force for good even while in prison.[11] His conscientious commitment to duty eventually placed him in the position of prime minister of Egypt, a platform he used to save the lives of thousands, including members of his family.

Proverbs advises us to make a similar commitment. "Go to the ant, you sluggard; consider its ways and be wise!"[12] The ant is a self-starter. It also prepares for winter during the productive days of summer. Those who want to avoid envy would do well to motivate themselves to diligence and perseverance. Don't wait for a supervisor to challenge you; encourage yourself. Don't wait for the storm clouds to gather before you prepare for the rain. Remember the laws of sowing and reaping—planting at the opportune time and reaping during the harvest. When we're fully engaged in pursuing the path that God has set before us, we have neither the time nor the inclination to be looking over the fence and coveting what our neighbor has.

FEARLESS PRINCIPLE: *Do not deviate from integrity*

Compromising our integrity is a dangerous game, pulling us away from the protection and favor to which the righteous are entitled.

"Surely, Lord, you bless the righteous; you surround them with your favor as with a shield."[13]

Psalm 34 reminds us that those who seek the Lord will not lack any good thing:

> Those who look to him for help will be radiant with joy;
>   no shadow of shame will darken their faces. . . .
> For the angel of the LORD is a guard;
>   he surrounds and defends all who fear him.
> Taste and see that the LORD is good.
>   Oh, the joys of those who take refuge in him!
> Fear the LORD, you his godly people,
>   for those who fear him will have all they need. . . .
> The eyes of the LORD watch over those who do right;
>   his ears are open to their cries for help. . . .
> The LORD hears his people when they call to him for help.
>   He rescues them from all their troubles.[14]

God promises to bless those who stay within the circle of his will. A good way to stay within that circle is to make personal resolutions. Jonathan Edwards, the great Christian preacher and writer, wrote more than sixty resolutions. One of them declared, "Resolved, never to do anything, which I should be afraid to do, if it were the last hour of my life."[15] He also resolved to live for God's glory. This kind of spiritual fitness will keep your feet on the right path.

David desired such spiritual fitness when he prayed to be delivered from deliberate sins—the kinds of transgressions that must be planned.[16] Inevitably, as we live, we commit various sins of omission and commission, doing what we shouldn't and failing to do what we should. But premeditated sin is especially offensive to God. Avoiding such presumptuous sins will keep us on the path of integrity.

FEARLESS PRINCIPLE: *Use adversity*

Joseph also persevered through setbacks, making constructive use of adversity. His fidelity to God landed him in prison after he was falsely accused of attempted rape. But Joseph didn't miss a beat, entering prison with such a positive attitude that opportunities soon emerged.

One important opportunity was the chance to interpret the dreams of Pharaoh's cupbearer and baker. Joseph reached out to them, ignoring the injustice he had endured and simply sought to serve them. This willingness to use his adversity for God's glory opened the door for Joseph to use his God-given talents to interpret their dreams. More than two years would pass before a new opportunity presented itself, yet Joseph never complained. Instead, he persevered through his disappointments. Those who would sidestep envy should do likewise.

FEARLESS PRINCIPLE: *Practice mercy*

What should we do when we have an opportunity to avenge a wrong that we have experienced? Joseph practiced mercy by forgiving his enemies. When his brothers arrived in Egypt, Joseph eventually revealed himself and provided them with a haven from the famine.

Joseph's mercy and grace didn't free his brothers from fear, for eventually their father, Jacob, would die.[17] When he did, Joseph's brothers felt understandable anxiety, uncertain whether Joseph would now avenge himself for their earlier envy and cruelty. But he had no desire to do so. He said to them, "You intended to harm me, but God intended it all for good."[18] Joseph saw the hand of God's providence in his brothers' envy, and he chose the quality of mercy over revenge.

We can choose mercy over retaliation because we trust God with our future. Instead of becoming victims of envy, we can walk away from it by believing that God will not permit dark forces to keep us from our ultimate destiny. We may not know what the future holds, but we can be confident that God holds our future. No matter how circuitous the road may seem, if we trust God, our final destination of fulfillment is certain.

Discovering our destiny and thriving in a threatening world require that we believe our sovereign God has our best interests at heart and that he intends to bring us to a desired end. We can avoid the pitfall of envy by following these guidelines:

- Expect trouble from unlikely sources.
- Develop a vigorous work ethic.
- Do not deviate from integrity.
- Use adversity.
- Practice mercy.

PURPOSEFUL PRAYER

God of our hopes and dreams, the center of our joy, deliver us from envy. Help us to trust you in times of adversity and prosperity, remembering that you will supply all of our needs. Help us to remember that we will reap a productive harvest if we persevere, never underestimating the power of your great name. Thank you that every good and perfect gift comes from you alone, for with you there is no variation or shadow of turning. We pray in your holy name. Amen.

CONCENTRATE
ON THE TASK

———— ✳ ————

LIVE A LESS COMPLICATED LIFE

THE WORDS TO THE SONG "Que Sera, Sera," made famous by singer Doris Day in the 1950s and 60s, capture the feeling that life is so complicated that there's little we can do about it. "Whatever will be, will be." Job puts it this way: "How frail is humanity! How short is life, how full of trouble!"[1] Jesus seemed to resonate with this sentiment when he said, "Here on earth you will have many trials and sorrows."[2]

How can we stay fearless in a world that seems to guarantee to every life the complications of misery and trial? Perhaps the answer is to stop believing that "whatever will be, will be" and to begin, with intentionality, to choose simplicity, the less-complicated road not often taken.

How do we choose simplicity? Hans Hofmann, a twentieth-century abstract expressionist painter, defined simplicity as "the ability . . . to eliminate the unnecessary so that the necessary may speak."[3] Can we do that? Can we eliminate the unnecessary in our lives, streamlining to the true essentials?

As I thought about choosing simplicity, my mind began to wander. I reflected on the time, now some forty-three years ago, when I brought my new bride to our first apartment. I had chosen the place without consulting with her, and she quickly noticed some other apartments nearby very similar to ours except with a balcony. She had to have that balcony, so I hired two teenagers from the church I pastored to help us move to a different apartment. We were able to move everything we owned in one trip with a pickup truck. Life was so much simpler then.

I have many friends who speak longingly of simpler times. Many of my political colleagues talk about the early days of their careers, when they had little money and no staff. Their spouses had to assist in the campaigning, knocking on doors and soliciting votes. "Chaplain," some have said, "those were the best years of our lives. I'd do anything to get them back. We had very little but were never happier."

I also remember when my son served as a Senate page. This is a program that permits eleventh graders to serve on Capitol Hill. They go to school, experiencing a very challenging academic program, but they also learn about the legislative process by running errands for senators. These often sleep-deprived high school students look very professional in their blue suits, white shirts, and blue ties. But I learned that their wardrobe was quite simple: They had only two suits that they alternated each day. What an interesting way to choose simplicity, to live a less complicated life.

Why is choosing simplicity so important? First, because it keeps us from being distracted by complexity. John Keble, a nineteenth-century British poet and songwriter, describes the importance of such a choice in his 1822 hymn, "New Every Morning Is the Love."

The trivial round, the common task,
will furnish all we ought to ask;
room to deny ourselves, a road
to bring us daily nearer God.[4]

In short, opportunities for spiritual encounters are often missed because we're distracted by complexity.

Choosing simplicity also keeps us from frittering away our lives. In *Walden*, Henry David Thoreau observes, "Our life is frittered away by detail. . . . Simplicity, simplicity, simplicity!"[5] What could you accomplish if you simplified your life until you majored in majors and minored in minors? I wrote a dissertation in less than a month when I eliminated the things that were frittering away my time. I once asked the late Senator Robert Byrd how he managed to write so many books. He straightened his back and said with stentorian intensity, "I don't watch television." If we are to live without fear in dangerous times, we must refuse to complicate our lives to the point that we fritter them away.

So how do we choose simplicity and declutter our lives?

FEARLESS PRINCIPLE: *Learn to say no*

Those who would choose simplicity must learn to slow things down, which means sometimes saying no. One of my dear friends, Ambassador Gilbert Robinson, gave me this sage advice: "Barry, as you get more visibility, more people will be after you. And it is now more important what you *do not* accept than what you accept."[6] This was an important admonition for me to hear, for I often had trouble saying no to speaking invitations, feeling that as one seeking to serve God, I should always say yes. I began to learn how to say no after hearing that Billy Graham had said that if he could live his life over, he would spend more time in study and reflection and less time traveling and speaking. In other words, he would choose a less-complicated life.

Learning to say no also helps us heed the biblical admonition to "make the most of every opportunity in these evil days."[7] How do we do that? We simply play catch-up. In a commencement speech at Florida A&M in 1960, then-president of Morehouse College and civil rights leader Benjamin Mays said, "The group that starts behind in the great race of life must forever remain behind or run faster than the race in front."[8] In other words, we must make up for life's deficits—both the ones we've inherited and the ones we've caused. As we learn to play catch-up, we'll find we have more time to use when we learn to say no.

FEARLESS PRINCIPLE:
Debunk the myth that more is better
When we choose the simplicity of a less-complicated life, we learn to debunk the myth that more is better. Jesus puts it this way in Luke 12:15: "Beware! Guard against every kind of greed. Life is not measured by how much you own." This is wonderful advice. How many times do we act as if more is better, forgetting that when we die we leave our wealth to others. Proverbs 11:4 reminds us that "riches won't help on the day of judgment." Millionaires die in spite of their abundance.

Knowing that less is often more is also important because more doesn't necessarily satisfy. Ecclesiastes 1:8 says, "No matter how much we see, we are never satisfied. No matter how much we hear, we are not content." Ultimately, *stuff* doesn't satisfy. That's why the apostle Paul advised Timothy, "If we have enough food and clothing, let us be content."[9] I suspect most of us would feel that such a short list of needs is unsatisfactory. Don't we also need a roof over our heads and other necessities? Nevertheless, Paul challenges us to choose a leaner simplicity.

When we learn that more isn't necessarily better, we will choose peace of mind over accumulating more stuff. As the writer of

Ecclesiastes says, "Better one handful with tranquility than two hand-fuls with toil and chasing after the wind."[10] That's a powerful verse. How many times in my life has the desire for that second handful kept me from experiencing contentment? And when I finally got the second handful, the stress and anxiety that accompanied it prompted me to question the wisdom of the quest to get it in the first place.

FEARLESS PRINCIPLE: *Appreciate what you have*

When we choose simplicity, we will begin to appreciate more the things we already have. If you're a person of faith, you may already possess more than you realize. For example, believers have been given the marvelous blessing of salvation, having been snatched from a predicament that could bring eternal ruin.[11]

As part of our salvation, we have been promised a place that has been prepared for us. Jesus said, "If it were not so, would I have told you that I go to prepare a place for you? And if I go and prepare a place for you, I will come again and will take you to myself, that where I am you may be also."[12] We also have a new status, for God calls us his sons and daughters.[13] And we have God's promise of power: "You will receive power when the Holy Spirit comes upon you. And you will be my witnesses, telling people about me everywhere."[14] God equips us with everything we need to fulfill his purpose.

God desires that we learn to appreciate what we have. In Colossians 3:1, we're admonished, "Since you have been raised to new life with Christ, set your sights on the realities of heaven, where Christ sits in the place of honor at God's right hand."

Do we really appreciate the blessings we already have? Do we delight in setting our sights on what lies ahead for us because we have an eternal life that has already begun? We really should begin to exemplify such gratitude because "wherever your treasure is, there the desires of your heart will be also."[15]

We should also remember that we are the owners of some precious promises from God. Romans 4:20-21 says, "Abraham never wavered in believing God's promise. . . . He was fully convinced that God is able to do whatever he promises." Do you have that kind of faith? Every promise of Scripture is yours and mine to claim. Peter calls them "great and precious promises," and says, "These are the promises that enable you to share [God's] divine nature and escape the world's corruption caused by human desires."[16] Have you claimed these blessings? God says, "I will open the windows of heaven for you. I will pour out a blessing so great you won't have enough room to take it in! Try it! Put me to the test!"[17]

FEARLESS PRINCIPLE: *Get alone*

Are you willing to sit alone in a quiet room? That's a skill and a discipline that you may need to learn if you're going to uncomplicate your life. In *Les Pensées*, Blaise Pascal, the French mathematician and philosopher, writes, "I have often said that all the misfortune of men [comes from] just one thing; that is, not knowing how to stay quietly in a room."[18] You can simplify your life by becoming comfortable with solitude. Psalm 46:10 puts it like this: "Be still, and know that I am God!"

Have you ever tried to cut back on busyness to simply be still? There was a time when I couldn't jog without earphones and music; I couldn't drive without the radio. Eventually, I learned the pleasure of simple meditation and reflection. I started by reflecting on Bible passages I had memorized, often discovering new insights by listening to my own thoughts. Later, I began taking twenty-minute breaks—closing my eyes and uttering a simple phrase, or sometimes a single word, that had spiritual significance to me. I discovered that during those twenty minutes the clutter of random thoughts disappeared, and I felt a wonderful tranquility. Meditation can be a great way to simplify your life.

This life of meditation is referred to in Psalm 1, which describes those who are blessed: "They delight in the law of the Lord, meditating on it day and night." Jesus, of course, was familiar with the Psalms, and they may have motivated him to spend time alone. Mark 1:35 describes the contemplative and solitary side of Jesus' life: "Before daybreak the next morning, Jesus got up and went out to an isolated place to pray." Likewise, as he prepared for his crucifixion, Jesus made his way to the garden of Gethsemane for some time alone in prayer.[19] Learn to appreciate the value of solitude; choose the simplicity of gathering strength by being alone.

One of the best ways I've found to spend my quiet time alone is to silently pray the Lord's Prayer found in Matthew 6:9-13. Nearly every person of faith knows this wonderful prayer by rote, but we shouldn't merely recite it; we should use it as an outline of themes to pray in our hearts. The opening words, *Our Father in heaven*, remind us that we don't need to extract gifts from God, but that we're praying to someone who delights to supply his children's needs. I know that his love for me is far greater than even what I feel for my own children, and it infuses me with a confidence that reassures me.

The request to "give us this day our daily bread" reminds us to pray for our present needs. How wonderful it is to lift our needs to someone who loves us more than we love ourselves. How vivifying it is to know that nothing that causes us anxiety is too small for God to notice or want to hear about. Once I prayed because I was concerned about whether I should shave my head—to achieve what I thought of at the time as the Michael Jordan look. It seemed like such a silly thing to bring before our sovereign God, but I did because it concerned me and reflected my present needs. Even as the manna that the children of Israel received each day in the wilderness was only enough for their daily needs, so our petitions should focus on our concerns in the here and now.[20]

When I pray, "Forgive us our debts, as we forgive our debtors," I'm reminded of my culpability in the sins of our nation and world.

I also begin to think about past sins, remembering that the best of us are sinners in the presence of a pure God. I sense my dependence upon God's mercy and grace, reveling in the salvation that He offers so freely and unconditionally.

When I pray, "Lead us not into temptation," I think about the many situations of testing I have faced, not merely in terms of seduction to do evil, but regarding those things that test my integrity, motives, commitment, and faithfulness. Focusing on future trials awakens in me holy desires and a greater determination not to disappoint God, who has done so much for me. We can simplify our lives by learning to creatively pray the Our Father.

FEARLESS PRINCIPLE: *Number your days*

In Psalm 90, Moses challenges us: "Teach us to number our days, that we may gain a heart of wisdom."[21] We are not to number our weeks, months, years, or decades; life is too fragile and brief. We're told to number our *days*. This suggests to me the importance of enjoying the spice of every day of life. Could it mean that we should live every day as if it were our last, because one day it will be?

A friend of mine decided not to make another run for office after a long career in public service. What he didn't know was that he had only eleven days left to live. While mourning my friend's death, I found myself troubled by the fact that the body doesn't seem to adequately forewarn us when we're reaching the end of life's journey. With only eleven days left to live, it seems that a small heads-up would be in order. But the Bible warns us, "Be ready all the time, for the Son of Man will come when least expected."[22] Could this possibly be another way of admonishing us to number our days?

When I sought to remind myself of life's brevity and to number my days, it had a wonderful effect on me. I found myself desiring to make a commitment to do something with my life that would have value in eternity. I wanted to leave the world better than I had found it by pursuing creative ways to let the oppressed go free. The words of Martin Luther King Jr.'s final sermon leaped to my mind: "If any of you are around when I have to meet my day, I don't want a long funeral. . . . I'd like somebody to mention that day that Martin Luther King Jr. tried to give his life serving others. I'd like for somebody to say that Martin Luther King Jr. tried to love somebody."[23] Numbering our days, and devoting ourselves to service and love, is truly a sentiment that will enable us to live less complicated lives.

FEARLESS PRINCIPLE: *Lighten up*

One of my friends went through a season of grief following his wife's death. For months he was immobilized by sorrow, staying by himself in a dark room, wrestling with his anguish. One morning, as the sunlight pierced the darkness of his bedroom, he sensed that God was about to communicate with him. Poised and ready for affirmation, comfort, and guidance, he waited for God to tell him what to do. Later he said to me, "Barry, it seemed as if I could sense God saying to me, 'Lighten up.'"

That certainly is one way to uncomplicate our lives: Lighten up. We cling to the past as we bear the burdens of the present and embrace the anxieties of the future. Lighten up. After all, Jesus said, "Do not be anxious about your life, what you will eat or what you will drink, nor about your body, what you will put on."[24] And Paul tells us in Philippians 4:6, "Don't worry about anything; instead, pray about everything." In short, lighten up.

We also have this astonishing command in 1 Thessalonians 5:16-18: "Always be joyful. Never stop praying. Be thankful in all circumstances, for this is God's will for you who belong to Christ Jesus." Lighten up. When we learn to major in things that really matter, we'll discover that our lives are simpler and more manageable.

Another way to lighten up is to learn to delegate some of our responsibilities. In Exodus 18:14, "When Moses' father-in-law saw all that Moses was doing for the people, he asked, 'What are you really accomplishing here? Why are you trying to do all this alone while everyone stands around you from morning till evening?'" Jethro's wise advice was for Moses to appoint group leaders who could "solve the people's common disputes. . . . Then you will be able to endure the pressures, and all these people will go home in peace."[25] Wise advice for lightening up.

Likewise, when the apostles were asked to take on more duties than they felt they could handle, they "gathered all the disciples together and said, 'It would not be right for us to neglect the ministry of the word of God in order to wait on tables. Brothers and sisters, choose seven men from among you who are known to be full of the Spirit and wisdom. We will turn this responsibility over to them.'"[26] We should lighten up by finding allies who can help us accomplish more than we could ever do alone.

FEARLESS PRINCIPLE: *Forget the past*

We can also uncomplicate our lives by practicing selective amnesia. In other words, forget the past. In Philippians 3:13-14, Paul writes, "I focus on this one thing: Forgetting the past and looking forward to what lies ahead, I press on to reach the end of the race and receive the heavenly prize for which God, through Christ Jesus, is calling us." With this strategy of leaving the past behind us, we can simplify our lives and stay fearless in a dangerous world.

What should you forget? For starters, we should forget past failures, for they do not define us. The apostle Paul had persecuted Christians and sought to have them killed, but he put that negativity behind him. Perhaps you have a checkered past like the woman who anointed the feet of Jesus at the house of the Pharisee, but she could worship Jesus without feeling intimidated because she had put the past behind her.[27] We should also forget past successes, not content to rest on our laurels, but always strive to accomplish more for God's Kingdom.

FEARLESS PRINCIPLE: *Walk with integrity*

Someone has said, "If you tell the truth, you don't have to remember what you said." This is one way of advising us to simplify our lives by walking with integrity. As it says in Proverbs, "Whoever walks in integrity walks securely, but whoever takes crooked paths will be found out."[28] Life is much easier and simpler when we walk with integrity.

Integrity simplifies living because the righteous are surrounded with the shield of God's favor.[29] This happens not only because God honors those who honor him, but also because of the laws of sowing and reaping.[30] The harvest is in the seeds, and we reap what we sow. Apple seeds bring apples, and pear seeds produce pears. Seeds always produce after their kind. Likewise, integrity brings a harvest of goodness and safety.

I once asked a friend on his ninety-second birthday, "What is the secret of living a long life?"

He responded, "You just have to live right."

Could it really be that simple? I think so. Those who walk with integrity walk securely. Integrity helps us ignore the bait of the evil one. Integrity prompts us to pass evil by on the other side of the road, allowing us to avoid the pathology that often comes at the harvest of transgression. Living right will shield us from a lot of unnecessary heartache and heartbreak. Integrity sows seeds that will bring a harvest of godliness and goodness.

FEARLESS PRINCIPLE: *Keep your eyes on the prize*

One of the popular songs of the civil rights movement was "Eyes on the Prize." One line says, "I know the one thing we did right was the day we began to fight; keep your eyes on the prize, hold on." When we have a prize, a goal, or a target, it certainly makes life less complicated. Paul stayed focused on the reward ahead of him. Learning that his execution was imminent, he declared, "The time for my departure is near. I have fought the good fight, I have finished the race, I have kept the faith. Now there is in store for me the crown of righteousness, which the Lord, the righteous Judge, will award to me on that day—and not only to me, but also to all who have longed for his appearing."[31]

———————

Setting goals is a good way to simplify our lives and choose integrity. Those who aim at nothing are bound to hit it every time, but goals enable us to channel our energy and time more wisely. They motivate us to keep our eyes on the prize. You can pursue simplicity and integrity by following these principles:

- Learn to say no.
- Debunk the myth that more is better.
- Appreciate what you have.
- Get alone.
- Number your days.
- Lighten up.
- Forget the past.
- Walk with integrity.
- Keep your eyes on the prize.

PURPOSEFUL PRAYER

God our refuge and strength, give us reverence for your greatness. May our awe of you lead us to the gate of true wisdom. Help us to submit to your plans, expecting you to direct our paths. Lord, give us the wisdom to choose simplicity, refusing to make life more complicated than it needs to be. May we receive your reproof for our tendency to complicate our lives unnecessarily, and may we cling to the knowledge that you chastise those whom you love for their own good. Sustain our hearts with your peace. We glorify your name. Amen.

STRIVE TO BELONG
TO GOD'S FAMILY

WHILE FLYING TO A SPEAKING ENGAGEMENT, I sat next to a physician who was a longevity expert. He pulled out his laptop and gave me his presentation on how to live a longer life. With a big smile, he said, "The true secret to a very long life is to choose the right parents." He went on to explain that genetics plays an important role in how long we can live, creating boundaries that are difficult to cross.

As I left the plane, I thought about the fact that we don't get to choose our parents. We have to play the genetic cards we're dealt at birth. Fortunately, we do get to choose our spiritual family. We get the chance to say yes to a God who offers us *eternal* life and who imprints upon our lives the "genetic" characteristics of his family.

So what should we do as we become members of this forever family?

FEARLESS PRINCIPLE:
Embrace your new family members

Far more important than our earthly relationships are the eternal relationships we become a part of when we join God's family. Ephesians 2:19 states, "You Gentiles are no longer strangers and foreigners. You are citizens along with all of God's holy people. You are members of God's family." What a wonderful declaration of a profound spiritual truth.

Before I became chaplain of the US Senate, I spent most of my adult life sailing the oceans and seas as a US Navy chaplain. Sometimes this meant being away from my wife and children for an agonizing six months or more at a time. How did I survive? I remembered that I belonged to a special household: the family of God. Wherever I traveled, I looked for a church, and there I found my family, regardless of the continent. I once spent Christmas with an Italian Christian family in Naples, and though I missed my own family at home, I was grateful to be part of the larger family of God, and I enjoyed the experience immensely.

This encounter with my new family members reminded me of Jesus' extended family. One time, as Jesus was preaching to a crowd of people, his mother and siblings showed up, concerned about his welfare.

> Someone told Jesus, "Your mother and your brothers are standing outside, and they want to speak to you."
>
> Jesus asked, "Who is my mother? Who are my brothers? Then he pointed to his disciples and said, "Look, these are my mother and brothers. Anyone who does the will of my Father in heaven is my brother and sister and mother!"[1]

Jesus made it clear that the members of God's family are joined by their allegiance and love for the Creator. We're still related by blood, but it is the blood of Christ's sacrifice.

First John 3:2 reminds us that you and I are sons and daughters of God, though we don't yet know what we will be like when time transitions into eternity. Nonetheless, Scripture assures us that "when Christ returns, we shall be like him, for we shall see him as he is."[2]

FEARLESS PRINCIPLE: *Be kind*

As members of God's household, we should strive to be kind, particularly to our own spiritual relatives. Second Samuel 9 chronicles a wonderful story about a time when King David arranged a compassionate and kind adoption. Saul and Jonathan had been killed in battle, and David had ascended to the throne. "One day David asked, 'Is anyone in Saul's family still alive—anyone to whom I can show kindness?'"[3]

This was a startling question. Typically when a king wanted to find out if anyone was still alive in the household of his predecessor, it was only so that he could have them killed and thus eliminate any threat to his reign. But that wasn't David's motivation at all.

When Saul's former servant Ziba said, "One of Jonathan's sons is still alive. He is crippled in both feet," David asked to have the young man brought to him.[4]

Jonathan's son Mephibosheth was brought to the palace, no doubt fearing for his life. But David told him not to be afraid. "I will restore to you all the land that belonged to your grandfather Saul, and you will always eat at my table."[5] Mephibosheth became a member of David's royal household because of the benevolence of a merciful king.

Isn't that what God has done for us? Like Mephibosheth, we, too, are lame, born in sin and shaped in iniquity.[6] But God sent his Son into the world to save us rather than condemn us.[7] He made it possible for us to be adopted, like Mephibosheth, into a royal family, making us his sons and daughters.

Isn't this also what God wants us to do for each other? Jesus said,

"As the Father has sent me, I am sending you."[8] He sends us into a dangerous world to do what he did while he was here. We are ambassadors for Jesus. As we seek to reconcile the world to him, we are to do this work with kindness.

FEARLESS PRINCIPLE: *Resemble your new family*

How can we know that we're members of God's household? In the Gospel of John, Jesus tells us about our distinctive family characteristic: "Your love for one another will prove to the world that you are my disciples."[9] Love is the identifying mark of the members of God's household. In fact, love is so important that Galatians 5:14 says, "The whole law can be summed up in this one command: 'Love your neighbor as yourself.'" We can keep the entire will of God by loving others as we love ourselves.

The greatest commandment is all about love. In Luke 10:25-29, a lawyer asks Jesus about the road to eternal life. Jesus replies, "What does the law of Moses say?"

The lawyer responds by quoting Deuteronomy 6:5: "You must love the Lord your God with all your heart, all your soul, and all your strength," and Leviticus 19:18: "Love your neighbor as yourself."

"Do this and you will live!" Jesus says. That's how important love is to God. In fact, Paul tells us in 1 Corinthians 13 that even if we were to give everything we had to the poor and even if we sacrificed our bodies in martyrdom, without doing these acts out of a heart of love, they would mean nothing.

Every year I go to my cousin's church in New Jersey to speak for Family and Friends Day. One year, he told me about a cousin of ours whom I hadn't met from South Carolina who was coming to the service and asked that I pick up Larry at the Philadelphia airport.

"What does he look like?" I asked. In fact, I asked the same question three times, and each time my cousin gave the same answer: "You'll have no problem picking him out of the lineup."

I drove toward New Jersey from Washington, DC, stopping at the Philadelphia airport to look for my cousin Larry. When I pulled up to the United Airlines arrival area, I saw someone who looked just like my aunt Honey. The family resemblance was unmistakable. I rolled down the window of my car and said, "You're Aunt Honey's boy."

He recognized me immediately and said, "And you look just like Aunt Tea." We both recognized the family resemblance. As Christians, our family resemblance is love. In this threatening world, we need to make sure that we resemble our new Christian family.

FEARLESS PRINCIPLE:
Find your place in the body and strive for unity
The Christian family is also known as "the body of Christ." As Paul says in Romans 12:5, "We are many parts of one body, and we all belong to each other." As members of this body, we should discover the abilities and talents we bring, "for the common good" or "so we can help each other."[10]

In order for the body to function properly, every member must do its part, and every part is important. "There are different kinds of spiritual gifts, but the same Spirit is the source of them all. There are different kinds of service, but we serve the same Lord. God works in different ways, but it is the same God who does the work in all of us. . . . Our bodies have many parts, and God has put each part just where he wants it. How strange a body would be if it had only one part! Yes, there are many parts, but only one body."[11]

Jesus desires that his body will function in unity. In his great intercessory prayer in John 17, he prays, "Father . . . I have given them the glory that you gave me, that they may be one as we are one . . . so that they may be brought to complete unity. Then the world will know that you sent me."[12] We are to work to unite the body of Christ and ensure that we stand as one in our threatening world.

FEARLESS PRINCIPLE: *Encourage one another*

Once we belong to God's family, we should become conduits of encouragement. The writer of Hebrews challenges us: "Encourage one another daily, as long as it is called 'Today,' so that none of you may be hardened by sin's deceitfulness."[13]

What kinds of words do we speak to other members of God's household? Proverbs 25:11 says, "A word fitly spoken is like apples of gold in a setting of silver."[14] When we speak appropriately to one another, words that are constructive and necessary, we fulfill our role as responsible members of God's household.

God expects us to encourage even wayward siblings and loved ones in his household. James says, "My dear brothers and sisters, if someone among you wanders away from the truth and is brought back, you can be sure that whoever brings the sinner back from wandering will save that person from death and bring about the forgiveness of many sins."[15] Now that's encouragement. Instead of writing off a wayward brother or sister, we should labor for his or her restoration. Encouragement and restoration are important ministries in a threatening world.

FEARLESS PRINCIPLE: *Join in your master's work*

As people of faith, we strive to belong to God's household in order to join his Son, Jesus, in his redemptive work. Ephesians 2:10 tells us, "God planned for us to do good things and to live as he has always wanted us to live. That's why he sent Christ to make us what we are."[16] And what are we? We are *sent ones*. As Jesus says in John 20:21, "As the Father has sent me, so I am sending you." We are ambassadors and agents of Christ, assisting him with the work he describes in Luke 4:18: "The Spirit of the Lord is upon me, for he has anointed me to bring Good News to the poor. He has sent me to proclaim that captives will be released, that the blind will see, that the oppressed will be set free, and that the time of the Lord's favor has come." When we join the family of God, we join a liberation movement, a cause far greater than ourselves.

Christ has chosen to use the members of his new household of faith to help him bring redemption to the world. He uses our efforts in a similar way as he did with his disciples in Matthew 10. Before he sent them "to cast out evil spirits and to heal every kind of disease," he challenged them: "Go and announce to them that the Kingdom of Heaven is near. Heal the sick, raise the dead, cure those with leprosy, and cast out demons. Give as freely as you have received!"[17] With the power of God at work in us, we can do the impossible. In this threatening world, we should strive to join him in his work.

FEARLESS PRINCIPLE: *Give yourself to God*

Before we give ourselves to any worthy endeavor, we must first give ourselves to God. This should be our first priority. Proverbs 23:26 declares, "Give me your heart. May your eyes take delight in following my ways." That's what God wants from us—not our money or our possessions; he wants the devotion of our hearts and the attention of our eyes. Using the Macedonian Christians as an example, the apostle Paul describes it this way: "They gave themselves first of all to the Lord, and then by the will of God also to us."[18] God wants every part of us, and he wants us to be available to serve according to his purpose.

In Luke 10, we find the story of two sisters, Mary and Martha, who sought to serve Jesus. Martha was a marvelous cook and worked assiduously to ensure that when Jesus paid a visit, he received the best hospitality. Mary took a different road. When Jesus visited, she didn't cook or entertain. Instead, she sat at Jesus' feet and gave him the gift of her undivided attention and love—the gift of herself. When Martha became upset that Mary wasn't helping to serve the meal, Jesus defended Mary, declaring that "Mary has chosen what is better, and it will not be taken away from her."[19]

A friend of mine has a stepdaughter who presented him with challenges as she grew up. She felt attached to her family of origin and resented much of the guidance and direction he tried to give her. As she grew older, they became closer. When his daughter reached adulthood, my friend received a wonderful surprise: She asked him to adopt her. She wanted to legally belong to his family. "You're the only father I've ever really known," she told him. "So we might as well make it official." With great joy, he made the adoption a reality.

When we come to truly know Jesus and realize that he is the best thing that has ever happened to us, we begin to strive to conform ourselves to the distinctive character of his family. This involves adhering to the following guidelines:

- Embrace your new family members.
- Be kind.
- Resemble your new family.
- Find your place in the body and strive for unity.
- Encourage one another.
- Join in your master's work.
- Give yourself to God.

PURPOSEFUL PRAYER

Almighty and loving God, we desire to be responsible members of your family. Rule in our hearts, keeping us from sin and sustaining our loved ones in all of their tomorrows. Surround us with the shield of your favor, as you provide us with a future and a hope, accomplishing in our lives more than we can ask or imagine. Make us your ambassadors in a threatening world. We praise your sovereign name. Amen.

CHANGE YOUR WORLD

WHAT ARE WE TO DO with our predatory world? If we're to stay
fearless in a dangerous environment, isn't it fair to ask to what end?
What is our purpose for being? Why did God permit us to come
into this world with our distinctive fingerprints and DNA? I believe
he desires for us to fulfill his purpose for our lives in our generation.
That's how the Bible sums up the life of King David: "When David
had served God's purpose in his own generation, he fell asleep; he
was buried with his ancestors and his body decayed."[1]

To fulfill God's purpose means participating in a relay race, receiving the baton from the preceding generation, running with it by
leaving the world better than we found it, and passing on the legacy
to those who follow us. Each generation has distinctive challenges.
We often refer to the World War II-era Americans as the Greatest
Generation, but in truth any generation with people who are faithful

to God's purpose for their lives is a great generation, one that has changed the world for the better.

God expects us to be world changers, to live lives that matter, to make someone or something different, ensuring that the world is a better place because we lived here. Martin Luther King Jr. once said, "If a man has not discovered something that he will die for, he isn't fit to live."[2] Jesus referred to the vital role we play in God's purpose when he said, "You are the salt of the earth. . . . You are the light of the world—like a city on a hilltop that cannot be hidden."[3] That's a pretty lofty order, but that's how God sees us.

Fortunately, we don't have to be salt and light for the planet in our own power. Acts 1:8 encourages us with these words: "You will receive power when the Holy Spirit comes upon you. And you will be my witnesses, telling people about me everywhere—in Jerusalem, throughout Judea, in Samaria, and to the ends of the earth." In short, we're empowered by the Spirit of God to be world changers.

So critical for our empowerment is the presence of the Holy Spirit that Jesus insisted his disciples wait for the arrival of this great Helper. Jesus said to his followers in his last visit with them, "Do not leave Jerusalem until the Father sends you the gift he promised, as I told you before. John baptized with water, but in just a few days you will be baptized with the Holy Spirit."[4]

We become world changers because God first changes us. "Anyone who belongs to Christ has become a new person. The old life is gone; a new life has begun!"[5] Just as a caterpillar becomes a butterfly through supernatural means, soaring over obstacles that once impeded its movements, so we are transformed. We soar over obstacles that once kept us earthbound. We're new creatures.

God initiates this metamorphosis. What Jesus said to his disciples applies to us: "You didn't choose me. I chose you. I appointed you to go and produce lasting fruit."[6] On another occasion, Jesus commented, "No one can come to me unless the Father who sent me draws them to me."[7] The apostle Paul told the members of the church at Philippi essentially the same thing: "God is working in you, giving you the desire and the power to do what pleases him."[8] Imagine that. We can't even *want* to do what's right without special help from God, who works through our wills.

How then do we become Spirit-filled world changers?

FEARLESS PRINCIPLE: *Receive the Holy Spirit's baptism*

To change the world in our generation, we need the Holy Spirit's help.[9] In Acts 19:2-3, the apostle Paul asks a group of Christian believers, "Did you receive the Holy Spirit when you believed? . . .

"No," they replied, "we haven't even heard that there is a Holy Spirit."

"Then what baptism did you experience?" he asked.

And they replied, "The baptism of John."

This reply was unsatisfactory, prompting Paul to enlighten them regarding the Holy Spirit's efficacy before rebaptizing them in the name of Jesus. "Then when Paul laid his hands on them, the Holy Spirit came on them."[10] That's how important the Holy Spirit's role is in making us world changers. The Holy Spirit's baptism is a gift we should eagerly anticipate.

The good news is that this baptism is a gift that is ours for the asking. Jesus said, "If you sinful people know how to give good gifts to your children, how much more will your heavenly Father give the Holy Spirit to those who ask him."[11]

FEARLESS PRINCIPLE: *Witness for your faith*

One of the key reasons for the Holy Spirit's baptism is to energize us to be witnesses for our faith. God isn't so much looking for theologians as he is for *witnesses*, people who can report what they have seen, heard, and experienced. D. T. Niles, a twentieth-century Sri Lankan evangelist, is reported to have said, "A Christian witness is not like a rich man who has a lot of bread which he hands out to the poor beggars who have nothing. He is rather like one beggar who tells another beggar where he has found bread."[12] How often we've felt inadequate in our efforts to witness. We don't know enough eschatology, soteriology, or ecclesiology. Fortunately, God isn't looking for scholars; he's looking for witnesses. You simply need to talk about what your eyes have seen, your ears have heard, and your heart has felt.

To be a witness also means being willing to give the last full measure of devotion in service. We must be prepared to die for our faith. The Greek word is *martus*, which refers to those who suffer death as a consequence of confessing Christ. The majority of Jesus' disciples were martyrs, demonstrating the greatest love by laying down their lives for a cause greater than themselves.

FEARLESS PRINCIPLE: *Focus on Jesus*

Jesus must be the focus of our witness.[13] Many weekends during the year, I preach somewhere away from home. When I enter a new church, the first thing I look for is a cross. I become nervous when I can't find a cross in a place of worship. I begin to wonder if there's an inadequate focus on Jesus, for the highest mountain in Christendom is Calvary. The cross is so special that Jesus once said of himself, "When I am lifted up from the earth, I will draw everyone to myself."[14]

Last year, I preached at a church that had no visible cross. I commented about this to the pastor and in my sermon, and when I was invited back this year, I was gratified to see they had added crosses on the wall behind the pulpit. I think that was God-honoring. "As for me," writes Paul to the Galatians, "may I never boast about anything except the cross of our Lord Jesus Christ."[15]

How Christ-centered is the worship in your church? A quote attributed to Charles Spurgeon, the great British preacher, goes something like this: "Start wherever you like in your sermon and head cross country as fast as you can toward Calvary."[16] Perhaps this is what the apostle Paul was attempting to do in his preaching when he declared, "I resolved to know nothing while I was with you except Jesus Christ and him crucified."[17] If the preaching, music, and liturgy in your church lack a Christ-centered emphasis, perhaps you should say something.

FEARLESS PRINCIPLE: *Begin witnessing at home*

In Acts 1:8, speaking to his disciples in Jerusalem, Jesus says that their witnessing would begin in Jerusalem. In other words, *at home.* Home is where the people who know us best reside; they aren't easily deceived. They test our ethical consistency in a way that outsiders can't. Family can be far more exacting than casual acquaintances. Perhaps Jesus was alluding to this challenge when he said, "A prophet is not without honor, except in his hometown."[18]

Jesus made this observation after returning home only to be greeted with skepticism by those who thought they knew him best. "Isn't he the carpenter, the son of Mary?" they asked.[19] "Where did he get such wisdom and the power to work these miracles?"[20]

Sadly, the skeptics missed a great opportunity, hindering the Lord's ministry. For Mark reports, "Because of their unbelief, he couldn't do any miracles among them except to place his hands on a few sick people and heal them."[21] Notice it says *couldn't,* not *wouldn't.* When it comes to witnessing, begin at home.

FEARLESS PRINCIPLE:
Cultivate an ever-widening circle of influence

We start at home with our witnessing, but we end by trying to influence the world. In the Great Commission, Jesus bids us to "go and make disciples of all the nations."[22] God expects our concentric circles of influence to embrace planet Earth. The Bible calls us Christ's ambassadors, through whom God is reconciling the world to himself.[23] Jesus said, "As the Father has sent me, so I am sending you."[24] The Father sent Jesus to save the world. We have been sent on the same mission.

Since the time of Christ, scores of Christians have left the comfort of home to take God's story of salvation to the world. William Carey went to India; Adoniram Judson to Burma; David Livingstone to Africa; George Müller to England; Hudson Taylor, Jonathan Goforth, and Eric Liddell to China; Amy Carmichael to India; Nate Saint and Jim Elliot to Ecuador. These missionaries were world changers who sought to fulfill Jesus' Great Commission for their generation.

———————

To sum it up, you and I should permit God to change our lives, transforming us into world changers who live fearlessly in a threatening world. We can prepare for this global mission by doing the following:

- Receive the Holy Spirit's baptism.
- Witness for your faith.
- Focus on Jesus.
- Begin witnessing at home.
- Cultivate an ever-widening circle of influence.

PURPOSEFUL PRAYER

Lord, make our lives productive for the glory of your name. Use us as your witnesses, and may our testimony begin at home. We wait in reverence before your throne to receive your guidance and follow your commands. Create in us clean hearts while renewing a right spirit within us. Help us today to discern your voice and do your will. We pray in your precious name. Amen.

START A CONSPIRACY
OF KINDNESS

ARE YOU GIVING UP on relationships? Have you become so frustrated by trying to make a positive difference in the lives of the people around you that you've simply held up the white flag of surrender? Maybe you need to start a conspiracy of kindness.

Most of us have an overly idealistic view of relationships. We want an Ozzie-and-Harriet marriage or a *Leave It to Beaver* parenting experience, based on two cheery television programs of the 1950s.

Honesty should compel us to admit that most relationships present challenges. Even biblical relationships left much to be desired. Adam and Eve's first son killed his younger brother, and Esau wanted to do the same to Jacob.[1] Jacob's sons later sold their brother Joseph into slavery.[2] David's son Amnon raped his half-sister Tamar in a fit of lust. In revenge, Tamar's brother Absalom murdered Amnon.[3] Throughout biblical history, relationships have been characterized by discord and pathology.

Secular history doesn't present a much more attractive picture. Particularly tragic is the history of warfare, as progressively more sophisticated weapons have killed more and more people. The casualties of war in the twentieth and twenty-first centuries alone are mind-boggling. According to some estimates, the American Civil War killed 628,000 people; as many as 20 million military and civilian deaths occurred in World War I; 60 million died in World War II; and the Chinese Cultural Revolution killed 40 million.[4] More recently, as many as 800,000 Tutsis were killed in a three-month period in 1994; more than 5 million people have perished in wars in the Congo; and the two American wars with Iraq destroyed an estimated half-million lives.[5] Whether you look at sacred or secular history, human beings have had a problem with relationships.

Why do we kill one another? James 4:1 suggests that wars result from our inner turmoil: "What is causing the quarrels and fights among you? Don't they come from the evil desires at war within you?" Perhaps the apostle Paul was referring to this inner turmoil when he declared, "I know that nothing good lives in me, that is, in my sinful nature. I want to do what is right, but I can't."[6] We fight one another because we're fighting ourselves. Our external conflict is but a manifestation of our internal unrest.

I think, however, that another more pressing reason exists for our pathetic relationships. In Ephesians, Paul reminds us of the presence of demonic forces: "We are not fighting against flesh-and-blood enemies, but against evil rulers and authorities of the unseen world, against mighty powers in this dark world, and against evil spirits in the heavenly places."[7] We often underestimate the power of satanic influence in our world. Jesus didn't make this mistake. In fact, he once referred to one of his closest disciples, Simon Peter, as "Satan."[8]

We have relationship problems because of jealousy, anger, and loss. If we're to stay fearless in this dangerous world, we must fight back by starting a conspiracy of kindness, which is simply a way of obeying the biblical command to "conquer evil by doing good."[9]

A *conspiracy* is simply acting in harmony toward a common goal, and *kindness* refers to being sympathetic or helpful. Kindness is a powerful force that can transform relationships. In fact, kindness is so powerful that we're given this counterintuitive advice in Proverbs 25:21-22: "If your enemies are hungry, give them food to eat. If they are thirsty, give them water to drink. You will heap burning coals of shame on their heads, and the Lord will reward you." Isn't that amazing? Our kindness can bring discomfiture to our enemies, perhaps even transforming them into our friends.

I remember wanting to hurt someone who had threatened me. I was in a position to keep this person from being promoted, and I eagerly anticipated the opportunity to do so. God's Spirit, however, prevailed in my heart, and I did the opposite of what I wanted. Months later, this person came to me with tears in his eyes. "Why are you being kind to me?" he said. "You're killing me!" It seems I had unintentionally heaped hot coals on his head.

What can we do to start a conspiracy of kindness?

FEARLESS PRINCIPLE: *Conquer anger*

The first key to spreading kindness is to conquer our anger. So many relationship problems are rooted in anger. That's why the writer of Proverbs says, "Whoever is slow to anger is better than the mighty, and he who rules his spirit than he who takes a city."[10] In other words, anger management is more important than might and power.

Sometimes our anger isn't directed at people, but at God. Jonah was angry when God didn't destroy the city of Nineveh, and God had to teach the prophet a valuable lesson. God caused a plant to grow up overnight, providing Jonah with some shade from the fierce heat of the noonday sun. But then God flipped the script and permitted the plant to die as quickly as it had grown, and Jonah was furious.[11] "Then God said to Jonah, 'Is it right for you to be angry because the plant died? . . . Nineveh has more than 120,000 people living in spiritual darkness. . . . Shouldn't I feel sorry for such a great city?"[12] Anger can hurt our relationships with each other and with God.

FEARLESS PRINCIPLE: *Conquer jealousy*

After we deal with anger, perhaps we should work at eliminating jealousy, too. Joseph's brothers wanted to kill him because he was their father's favorite son, and Jacob foolishly lavished preferential favors on him. He gave Joseph a coat of many colors, which his brothers deeply resented. Moreover, Joseph was a dreamer who made no attempt to keep his ambitions to himself. His brothers hated the fact that one of Joseph's dreams seemed to indicate that he would one day rule over them.[13] If we're to start a conspiracy of kindness, we must deal with our jealousy.

FEARLESS PRINCIPLE: *Conquer the demonic*

Why are people sometimes angry and sometimes jealous? In Matthew 13:24-28, Jesus tells the story of a man who planted good seeds in a field. Unfortunately, an enemy came along and planted weeds in the same field. When the harvest time arrived, the man's servants noticed the weeds and said to their master, "The field where you planted that good seed is full of weeds! Where did they come from?"

The master responded, "An enemy has done this!" And by *enemy*, Jesus was referring to the devil.

The apostle Peter later picked up on this theme, declaring that the devil was an adversary "looking for someone to devour."[14] After his experience of denying Jesus and being "sifted" by Satan, Peter was particularly sensitive to the "strategies of the devil."[15] Those who would commence a conspiracy of kindness will be aware of and strive to conquer the demonic.

FEARLESS PRINCIPLE: *Conquer verbal abuse*

Be sensitive to the danger signals of verbal abuse. Matthew 12:34 reminds us that "whatever is in your heart determines what you say." What comes out of our mouths is instructive. For example, as a person of faith, if in rush-hour traffic I find myself regressing to the use of profanity, it should be a danger signal. It may mean that I've been neglecting my devotional life or listening to the wrong kind of music or viewing the wrong kind of movies. My uncharacteristic use of profanity should raise a red flag for me spiritually.

I once had a counselee who came to me because her boyfriend had used a derogatory word to describe her. "Should I be concerned about this, Chaplain Black?" she asked.

"I have a question for you," I responded. "If he calls you that when you're his fiancée, what do you think he'll call you after you're married?" Proverbs 18:21 says, "The tongue can bring life or death." We should evaluate our speech to help us gauge our level of spiritual and ethical fitness.

What should be the goal of speaking for a person of faith? The apostle Paul offers us guidance: "Do not let any unwholesome talk come out of your mouths, but only what is helpful for building others up according to their needs, that it may benefit those who listen."[16] Isn't that powerful? The goal of my speaking is to be helpful and to build up other people. So before I open my mouth to speak, I should ask myself two critical questions: (1) Will what I say be helpful? (2) Will it build up those who hear me? Perhaps Proverbs 25:11 is referring to the power of words when it states, "A word fitly spoken is like apples of gold in a setting of silver."[17]

Sadly, we sometimes underestimate the power of words. We say, "Sticks and stones may break my bones, but words will never hurt me." But this isn't necessarily true. Sigmund Freud once observed:

Words were originally magic, and the word retains much
of its old magical power even to-day. With words, one man
can make another blessed, or drive him to despair; by words
the teacher transfers his knowledge to the pupil; by words
the speaker sweeps his audience with him and determines
its judgments and decisions from teacher to student;
words enable the orator to sway his audience and dictate
its decisions. Words call forth effects and are the universal
means of influencing human beings.[18]

Do your words build people up? Don't underestimate the power of
what you say.

David and Jonathan possessed one of the greatest friendships in
recorded history. In 1 Samuel 23:15-29, we see the power of words
in their friendship as Jonathan's encouragement helps David survive seasons of distress and grief. Though Jonathan was heir to the
throne of Israel, he believed that God's hand was on David. "'Don't
be afraid,' Jonathan reassured him. 'My father will never find you!
You are going to be the king of Israel, and I will be next to you.'"[19]
The two men made a covenant of friendship between themselves
and God, starting a conspiracy of kindness. Jonathan's kind words
helped build up David so that he didn't become weary in doing what
was right.

Many years ago, I did the opposite of Jonathan. I was with a
young lady on an unofficial date at a restaurant. After I bought her
a glass of orange juice for breakfast, she said, "That was so generous
and kind of you." Not wanting her to think I had romantic intentions just because I paid for the juice, I quickly replied, "It's no big
deal. I would do the same thing for a beggar in need." Needless to say,
those words were neither kind nor helpful. They tore down rather
than built up.

Now here's what may surprise you: Even after I made that terrible statement—more than forty years ago—that young lady agreed to marry me, though she still reminds me of the incident from time to time. (I thought the statute of limitations would have run out by now, but apparently not.)

The Bible reminds us that one day we'll be accountable to God for every idle word we speak.[20] How critically important then that our words enliven and invigorate, rather than discourage and tear down.

FEARLESS PRINCIPLE: *Strengthen racial relationships*
As Martin Luther King Jr. once observed, "I think it is one of the tragedies of our nation, one of the shameful tragedies, that eleven o'clock on Sunday morning is one of the most segregated hours, if not *the* most segregated hours, in Christian America."[21] Even with the progress we've made as a nation since 1960, perhaps that can still be said. For most of my life as a Christian, I have worshiped in a segregated setting. Sadly, I have rarely even thought about reaching out to witness to someone of a different race, even when I worked as an evangelist.

How well are we doing as the body of Christ in strengthening race relations? We mustn't stop too soon in our quest to bring unity to the family of faith across racial, ethnic, and social boundaries. May we undertake a conspiracy of kindness that touches all of humanity.

The twentieth century was indeed a time of racial and ethnic division and conflict. The world witnessed the Nazi extermination of Jews, Gypsies, and other "undesirables." African nations threw off the yoke of colonialism, and a civil rights movement was ignited in America. With the disintegration of the Soviet Union, we saw ethnic conflicts flair up in Ukraine and the former Yugoslavia. And in 1995, French Canadians in Quebec came within a few parliamentary votes of separating from the rest of Canada. It is difficult to ignore the impact of ethnicity in our world.

With changing demographics, things don't necessarily improve, and we're often tempted to abandon hope of igniting a conspiracy of kindness when it runs up against racial and ethnic lines. Nonetheless, we have a responsibility to break down barriers that divide us, for "there is no longer Jew or Gentile, slave or free, male and female. For you are all one in Christ Jesus."[22]

In the Gospel of John, we see Jesus strengthening a cross-cultural relationship: "When a Samaritan woman came to draw water, Jesus said to her, 'Will you give me a drink?' . . . The Samaritan woman said to him, 'You are a Jew and I am a Samaritan woman. How can you ask me for a drink?' (For Jews do not associate with Samaritans.)"[23] We can see how Jesus took the initiative in bringing a conspiracy of kindness to this woman. He proceeded to tell her about living water, awakening in her a sense of spiritual need and desire. Sidestepping the distraction of a theological debate, he empowered this Samaritan to witness to others about how Christ had transformed her life. If Jesus so meticulously reached out to someone of a different culture to strengthen that relationship, shouldn't we follow his wonderful example and start our own conspiracies of kindness?

FEARLESS PRINCIPLE: *Practice God's presence*
Practicing God's presence will help you sustain your conspiracy of kindness. How can you begin to practice God's presence? Start by attempting to be aware that God is with you always. When you're driving to work, remember that he is in the car with you. When you're involved in a morning meeting, know that he is there to give you needed wisdom. When you find yourself forgetting about his presence, immediately refocus. You'll find that, at first, your awareness of God's presence may be for only a few minutes; then you'll forget and have to refocus. With practice, however, you'll soon discover that the time of your awareness of God's immanence will lengthen, and several hours may fly by as you maintain a palpable awareness

of God's nearness. This awareness will bring great joy to your life, enabling you to continue your conspiracy of kindness.

FEARLESS PRINCIPLE: *Learn to forgive*

A critical part of any conspiracy of kindness is learning to forgive. Ephesians 4:32 reminds us to "be kind to each other, tenderhearted, forgiving one another, just as God through Christ has forgiven you." Our willingness to forgive others should be linked to our gratitude for God's willingness to forgive us. In the Lord's Prayer, we're instructed to pray, "Forgive us our debts, as we also have forgiven our debtors."[24]

In Matthew 18, Jesus tells a story about forgiveness, about a servant who owed his master a great sum, far more than he could pay. When the man was about to be thrown into debtor's prison, he pleaded so piteously for forgiveness that the master expunged the debt. When the forgiven debtor left his master, he encountered a fellow servant who owed him a fraction of what he had once owed. Instead of showing his friend mercy and forgiveness in keeping with his master's example, "he grabbed him by the throat and demanded instant payment."[25] When his master heard what the servant had done, he angrily reversed his forgiveness of the debt. When we remember the great debt we owe to God and how he has forgiven us, we're in no position to refuse forgiveness to others.

Why are we often so reluctant to forgive? Sometimes it's because we're angry. We're like Esau, who was still angry with Jacob after twenty years.[26]

A second reason we're reluctant to forgive is a desire to satisfy our sense of justice. In the parable of the prodigal son, the elder brother is reluctant to forgive his wayward brother, even though their father has shown mercy. He says, "When this son of yours comes back after squandering your money . . ."[27]

Notice he doesn't say "my brother," but "this son of yours." He wanted justice served, not mercy.

We also can be reluctant to forgive because the person who hurt us is sometimes in denial, refusing to admit to any wrongdoing. How do we forgive someone who doesn't take responsibility or show repentance?

Or we may be unwilling to forgive because the transgression is habitual. It was probably such an offender that Peter thought about when he asked Jesus, "How often should I forgive someone who sins against me? Seven times?"[28]

Perhaps the most human reason for being reluctant to forgive is that we want revenge. We want to harm as we have been harmed, the old "eye for an eye and tooth for a tooth" philosophy.

No one demonstrated a willingness to forgive more than Jesus. In Luke 23:34, while he was being crucified, he prayed, "Father, forgive them, for they don't know what they are doing." If Jesus could pray for the people who crucified him, what excuse can we possibly offer for failing to forgive? Jesus' willingness to pray for his enemies reminds us to acknowledge, when we can, the blindness of the human heart. Sometimes, even when we sin against others, we do so in ignorance—mistakes of the head and not the heart.

Another great example is found in Acts 7 at the death of Stephen, the first Christian martyr. As a cruel mob pelts him with rocks until he dies, his final prayer is a request to God for mercy: "Lord, do not hold this sin against them."[29]

If we are to love our enemies, do good to those who hate us, bless those who curse us, and pray for those who mistreat us,[30] we certainly must learn how to forgive others in the same way that God has forgiven us. If we want to remain fearless in a dangerous world, we can start a conspiracy of kindness by following these guidelines:

- Conquer anger.
- Conquer jealousy.
- Conquer the demonic.
- Conquer verbal abuse.
- Strengthen racial relationships.
- Practice God's presence.
- Learn to forgive.

PURPOSEFUL PRAYER

Our Father, bless our efforts to start a conspiracy of kindness. Give us the ability to differentiate your guidance from all others, permitting you to lead us to your desired destination. Speak to us through your Word, guiding us with your Spirit and sustaining us with your might. Today, descend on our hearts, for apart from you we can do nothing. We put our trust in you. Amen.

PERSEVERE
THROUGH
REJECTION

✴

DEAL WITH BROKEN DREAMS

MY FRIEND CLARK was the life of the party. Always smiling, he possessed a seemingly unstoppable optimism. His cheerful outlook and quick wit made him a joy to be near. I anticipated his clever quips and felt the energy he brought into every room he entered. One day, however, things were different, and Clark seemed to be walking beneath dark clouds of depression. Then I found out he had just learned that his name wasn't on the latest promotion list. This was devastating news for a career military officer.

"Clark, I'm sorry to hear the bad news," I heard myself say—instantly regretting the clumsiness of my comment. "If there's anything I can do for you, please let me know." Again, I regretted my bland and clichéd words as soon as they left my mouth. Clark nodded solemnly, kindly acknowledging my discomfort.

But what can we do when our dreams lie broken at our feet? How can we handle shattered aspirations when they belong to us or someone we care about? What should we do when we know that our fondest hopes will never be realized? To stay fearless in a dangerous world, we must learn to deal with broken dreams.

How desperately our world needs dreamers. Without visionary people, the world is less safe. In the language of the King James Version, "Where there is no vision, the people perish."[1] Those who experience thoughts, images, and sensations during slumber have often blessed humanity, seeing things that never were and asking, Why not?[2] They also, however, sometimes see their dreams deferred, dried up like a raisin in the sun. Like Moses, they never get to the Promised Land, only seeing it from afar.

Is there a strategy for dealing with broken dreams and staying fearless in a dangerous world?

FEARLESS PRINCIPLE: *Live intentionally*

How goal-oriented are you? If we're going to deal with broken dreams in a predatory world, we must live with intentionality. As the saying goes, those who fail to plan, plan to fail. Jesus was goal-oriented, hitting targets for outreach, ministry, and evangelism throughout his life. As he prepared for his triumphal entry into Jerusalem on Palm Sunday, he gave his disciples the following instructions: "Go to the village ahead of you, and as you enter it, you will find a colt tied there, which no one has ever ridden. Untie it and bring it here."[3] Jesus lived with intentionality, and he had a plan.

Jesus also expects us to live intentionally. He said, "Who would begin construction of a building without first calculating the cost to see if there is enough money to finish it?"[4] Have you counted the cost of following Jesus? How well planned is your life? Have you ever thought of the things you would like people to say at your funeral? Perhaps the time has come for some goal setting, for "living on purpose" so that there will be positive things that can be said about you. Those who aim at nothing hit it every time.

FEARLESS PRINCIPLE: *Live with courage*

Jesus knew something about broken dreams. On the night of his betrayal, he knew that one disciple would betray him for thirty pieces of silver and another would deny him three times before the rooster crowed.[5] Before that fateful night, Jesus had ridden from the Mount of Olives into Jerusalem with an entourage of unarmed disciples. He and his followers were buoyed by a crowd who danced and shouted, "Blessed is the King who comes in the name of the Lord!"[6] This ride of Christ's was courageous, for he knew that the Romans' chief Jerusalem garrison, the Tower of Antonia, was nearby, and that Gentile soldiers watching his procession might oppose his parade and decide to use repressive measures to express their displeasure. In spite of the risk, Jesus courageously made his triumphal entry into the city, knowing that those who celebrated him that day might also back his crucifixion later that week.

Are you living boldly? Is your journey characterized by courage? Can you say with the apostle Peter, "Lord, if it's really you, tell me to come to you, walking on the water"?[7] If it is indeed Jesus, why wouldn't you step out of the boat of your quiet desperation at his bidding? Why would you live a pedestrian life when you can experience far more fulfillment with the life of faith? Why wouldn't you stay fearless in a dangerous world?

David knew something about living with courage. When all of Israel's army trembled before the bellicose rhetoric of Goliath, David accepted the challenge to fight the giant, living above cowardice.[8] He had shown similar courage earlier in his life when he killed a lion and a bear that attacked his small flock of sheep. I would have had a problem with risking my life for a few sheep, but David lived courageously. Those who learn to thrive in a dangerous world will discover strategies for courageous living.

FEARLESS PRINCIPLE: *Find guidance in God's Word*

Where did Jesus get the idea to make his triumphal entry into

Jerusalem? Could it have been that he knew the messianic prophecy of Zechariah 9:9: "Rejoice, O people of Zion! Shout in triumph, O people of Jerusalem! Look, your king is coming to you. He is righteous and victorious, yet he is humble, riding on a donkey—riding on a donkey's colt."

Jesus received his inspiration and guidance from Scripture. In the wilderness of temptation, he had earlier declared, "People do not live by bread alone, but by every word that comes from the mouth of God."[9] Three times in that same wilderness, he responded to the devil's overtures to sin by quoting Scripture. God's Word was truly a lamp for his feet and a light for his path.[10]

FEARLESS PRINCIPLE: *Trust God's sovereignty*

Jesus stayed strong in his predatory environment by trusting God's sovereignty. He taught us to pray, "Your kingdom come, your will be done, on earth as it is in heaven."[11] He was so convinced that he was a part of the unfolding of God's loving providence that he said, "I carry out the will of the one who sent me, not my own will."[12] His last words from the cross, after being ravaged by his enemies, were, "Father, into your hands I commit my spirit."[13]

Often when we face devastating circumstances, we're tempted to say, "Why me?" Wouldn't it be better to declare with Job, "[God] knows the way that I take; when he has tested me, I will come forth as gold"?[14] Why not trust God's sovereignty?

The fact is, as people of faith we can be assured that God is in charge of our lives. Psalm 37:23 tells us that "the Lord directs the steps of the godly." Not just the overall journey, but the steps.

Proverbs 3:5-6 reiterates this principle, reminding us that God directs the paths of those who trust in him and seek to do his will.

We can trust God's sovereignty even in a dangerous world because he sees our lives at a glance—past, present, and future. Nothing surprises him. He said to Jeremiah, "I knew you before I formed you in your mother's womb. Before you were born I set you apart and appointed you as my prophet to the nations."[15] Imagine that. Before Jeremiah was conceived, God already had a challenging plan for his life. We can trust God to bring us to a desired destination by following his providential leading.

FEARLESS PRINCIPLE: *Submit to God's will*

If we trust God's sovereignty, we should be willing to submit to his will. Jesus demonstrated this marvelously in the garden of Gethsemane. Realizing that the time had come for him to die for humanity, he prayed this simple prayer: "Father, if you are willing, please take this cup of suffering away from me. Yet I want your will to be done, not mine."[16] In our dangerous world, it's in our enlightened self-interest to submit ourselves to God's plan instead of pushing for our own.

Shadrach, Meshach, and Abednego discovered the blessings that can come from submission to God's will. Faced with the prospect of being executed by King Nebuchadnezzar for refusing to bow to an idol the king had erected on the plain of Dura, these young men declared, "If we are thrown into the blazing furnace, the God whom we serve is able to save us. He will rescue us from your power, Your Majesty. But even if he doesn't, we want to make it clear to you, Your Majesty, that we will never serve your gods or worship the gold statue you have set up."[17] These boys were so intent on doing God's will that they chose to burn rather than bow, and thus they experienced the joy of a miraculous deliverance from what seemed like certain death. In this precarious world, learn to say to God, "May your will be done."

FEARLESS PRINCIPLE: *Embrace opposition*

Staying fearless in a dangerous world requires that we embrace opposition. During his triumphal entry into Jerusalem, Jesus was accosted by some religious leaders who said, "Teacher, rebuke your disciples and tell them to stop this loud celebration."[18] These leaders were fearful that the loud worship might cause trouble with the Roman soldiers who were tasked with keeping the peace, but Jesus embraced this opposition and said to his detractors, "If my disciples and followers don't passionately praise God, the rocks will cry out."[19]

It becomes easier to embrace opposition when we remember the parable of the soils in Matthew 13. The farmer planted his seeds, but 75 percent of his efforts went to waste, falling on unproductive soil. Nonetheless, he kept on planting until his seeds began to hit good soil and brought forth an exponential harvest—thirty-, sixty-, and one hundredfold. And so it is with life. We must continue to plant in spite of the obstacles, embracing the opposition and claiming God's promise that if we don't faint, we will reap a bountiful harvest in due season.[20]

You and I can deal with broken dreams and stay fearless in a dangerous world. We need simply to follow this blueprint:

- Live intentionally.
- Live with courage.
- Find guidance in God's Word.
- Trust God's sovereignty.
- Submit to God's will.
- Embrace opposition.

PURPOSEFUL PRAYER

Eternal Father, help us to walk in your ways, keeping your precepts with such integrity that we can deal with broken dreams in this dangerous world. Grant that we will never be ashamed. Incline our hearts to your wisdom, providing us with the understanding we need to accomplish your purposes in our world. Let your mercy protect us from life's dangers, as we learn to find delight in your commandments. We pray in your powerful name. Amen.

26

SEIZE LIFE'S SECOND CHANCES

WE ARE OFTEN LESS MERCIFUL with each other than God is with us. Many times, we are reluctant to forgive those who have offended us, although we're routinely the beneficiaries of God's mercies and forgiveness. King David understood that people can be less forgiving than God. When given the option of receiving punishment from God or from his enemies, David responded, "Let us fall into the hands of the Lord, for his mercy is great. Do not let me fall into human hands."[1] David knew that if he were to receive a second chance at abundant living, it would come from God and not humanity.

Are you willing to seize the second chances that God offers you? In John 8, we encounter a woman caught in adultery who is brought to Jesus and receives a second chance. Her accusers want her stoned to death, but Jesus will have none of that: "Let the one who has never sinned throw the first stone!"[2] This woman escapes execution by the mercy of God and is given an opportunity to seize life's second chance. Her story shows us how we can do the same.

God is more willing to give us second chances than we are to receive them: "As surely as I live, says the Sovereign Lord, I take no pleasure in the death of wicked people. I only want them to turn from their wicked ways so they can live. Turn! Turn from your wickedness, O people of Israel! Why should you die?"[3]

A similar sentiment is expressed in John 3:17: "God sent his Son into the world not to judge the world, but to save the world through him." Each of us should prepare to seize God's second chances, for his mercy is "from everlasting to everlasting."[4] Stay fearless in a dangerous world by seizing God's second chances. Here are a few suggestions on how to do it.

FEARLESS PRINCIPLE: *Reject hypocrisy*

The religious leaders in John 8 who brought the adulterous woman to Jesus did so with hypocritical motives, seeking to trap him. They said to him, "This woman was caught in the act of adultery. The law of Moses says to stone her. What do you say?"[5] John 8:6 reveals their hypocritical motives: "They were trying to trap him into saying something they could use against him."

Hypocrisy can keep us from seizing life's second chances. It can keep us in a state of denial so that we refuse to admit we need help. Judas, the disciple who betrayed Jesus, was afflicted with the disease of hypocrisy. When Mary came to Simon's feast and anointed Jesus with expensive ointment, Judas responded by saying, "That perfume was worth a year's wages. It should have been sold and the money given to the poor."[6] But John, an observant fellow disciple, adds a bit of insight about Judas: "Not that he cared for the poor—he was a thief, and since he was in charge of the disciples' money, he often stole some for himself."[7] Clearly, his condemnation of Mary's generosity was the height of hypocrisy. We should strive to be real and reject hypocrisy.

FEARLESS PRINCIPLE: *Err on the side of mercy*

How often we fail to show mercy—even though the Bible tells us that the merciful will be shown mercy.[8] Micah 6:8 says that God requires us to "do what is right . . . love mercy, and . . . walk humbly" with him. How often do we err on the side of mercy?

The people who took the adulterous woman to Jesus were themselves sinners, yet they used her as a pawn in their plan to trap Jesus. They failed to love mercy or show it.

Jonah failed to err on the side of mercy. He became angry because God didn't destroy the city of Nineveh.[9] God taught Jonah an object lesson about mercy, permitting a plant to spring up overnight, protecting the prophet's head from the heat of the sun. But the plant died almost as soon as it appeared, and Jonah was angry again.

"You're angry," God said to him, "because of the death of a single plant, but you're not upset that 120,000 people were living in spiritual darkness and could have been killed."[10] In other words, *Where are your feelings of mercy?* We need to major in mercy and minor in judgment.

FEARLESS PRINCIPLE: *Love people and use things*

We usually reverse this equation, using people and loving things. Galatians 5:14 condenses the message of the entire Bible into a single verse: "The whole law can be summed up in this one command: 'Love your neighbor as yourself.'" In short, if we want to bring theological insight to bear on any ethical conundrum, we can start by discovering how the issue is connected to loving others as we love ourselves. Who among us would ever have had a second-chance opportunity without receiving God's unconditional love?

FEARLESS PRINCIPLE:
Judge yourself before condemning others

Jesus said to those who wanted the adulterous woman to die, "Let the one who has never sinned throw the first stone!"[11] In other words, those who live in glass houses shouldn't walk around without clothing. The woman's accusers were hoist with their own petard, for they knew sin up close and personal, compelling them to steal quietly away.

After a prominent evangelist helped to have a colleague defrocked and forced to leave active ministry because of sexual misconduct, the defrocked colleague hired a private detective to follow his accuser around. He soon discovered that the accuser was also engaging in sexual misconduct. How easy it is for us to see the sins in others. Remember, whenever you point your finger at someone else, three fingers are pointing back at you. Judge yourself before you condemn someone else.

FEARLESS PRINCIPLE: *Trust God's confidence in you*

One of the most remarkable things about this story is Jesus' confidence in the adulterous woman. He says to her, "Go now and leave your life of sin."[12] He wouldn't have asked the woman to do something that he would not enable her to do, for his biddings are empowered. When he said to a man with a withered hand, "Stretch out your hand," the man could not accomplish this impossible request without supernatural help, and Jesus provided exactly that.[13] Jesus has more confidence in you than you have in yourself, so embrace his optimistic outlook for your future, seize your second chance, and stay fearless in a dangerous world.

FEARLESS PRINCIPLE:
Respond positively to God's goodness

It is God's goodness that leads us to repentance, so don't fight the feeling. Instead, respond positively to his overtures of grace.[14] The apostle Paul says that "Christ's love compels us, because we are convinced that one died for all."[15] Let your gratitude for God's gift of salvation strengthen you to resist temptation.

From time to time, when I'm tempted to give in to a besetting sin, I pause and reflect on my life. I remember the many times I have yielded to that particular transgression and disappointed my Lord. Striving to live in a day-tight compartment, I make a commitment to resist that temptation—not always, but just for today. I know the joy that my small efforts will bring to my Savior, who has done so much more for me. His love compels me to resist the tempter. When love motivates me, resisting the enemy of my soul becomes easier. Each of us should strive to respond positively to God's goodness.

FEARLESS PRINCIPLE: *Make forgiveness a habit*

Because we have been forgiven, we should be willing to make a habit of forgiving. "Forgive us our debts, as we also have forgiven our debtors."[16] Peter, who knew this prayer, asked Jesus, "How often should I forgive someone who sins against me? Seven times?"[17]

"'No, not seven times,' Jesus replied, 'but seventy times seven!'"[18] In other words, make forgiveness a habit. When I think of the enormity of the things for which God has forgiven me, it becomes difficult for me not to desire a forgiving spirit.

FEARLESS PRINCIPLE: *Comprehend your true glory*

In Luke 10, when the seventy-two disciples returned from their foray into a dangerous world, they were radiant with joy. Though they had been sent as lambs in the midst of wolves, their successes had exceeded every expectation. They had prepared to be sent, facing the realities of the dangers, wise as serpents and harmless as doves. They had not cluttered their lives with material things but had concentrated on their tasks, persevered through rejection, and met many needs. And now they "joyfully reported" to Jesus, "Lord, even the demons obey us when we use your name!"[19]

Jesus responded and reminded them to comprehend their true

glory: "'Yes,' he told them, 'I saw Satan fall from heaven like lightning! Look, I have given you authority over all the power of the enemy, and you can walk among snakes and scorpions and crush them. Nothing will injure you. But don't rejoice because evil spirits obey you; rejoice because your names are registered in heaven."[20]

Jesus warned his disciples against pride and overconfidence. Yes, they had been given remarkable power to thrive in a threatening world, but their greatest and truest glory was that their names were inscribed in heaven. Our truest glory is not what we have done for God in a dangerous world, but what he has done for us.

When we seize life's second chances, we comprehend our true glory. Remember, "it is God who works in you, both to will and to work for his good pleasure."[21] He keeps us fearlessly thriving in a threatening world.

Stay fearless in a dangerous world; seize life's second chances by following these principles:

- Reject hypocrisy.
- Err on the side of mercy.
- Love people and use things.
- Judge yourself before condemning others.
- Trust God's confidence in you.
- Respond positively to God's goodness.
- Make forgiveness a habit.
- Comprehend your true glory.

PURPOSEFUL PRAYER

Infinite Holy Spirit, whose love is broader than the measure of our minds, thank you for enabling us to live fearlessly in a threatening world. We rejoice that your mercy extends to all people, even when we walk on life's dangerous paths. Let your peace be within our hearts as you calm our restless strivings. Destroy our fears with the knowledge of your providential care that prevails even when we walk through the valleys of the shadows.

Lord, we pray for all who are in peril. Protect all whose work brings them into dangerous situations. We pray also for those who have failed in noble efforts and who are in danger of giving up the good fight. We ask you to sustain those whose fear of tomorrow renders them useless today. Keep us ever aware of the dangers that lurk in the paths of success and failure, defeat and triumph alike. May we continue to find encouragement in the words of Psalm 46:

> *God is our refuge and strength,*
> > *always ready to help in times of trouble.*
> *So we will not fear when earthquakes come*
> > *and the mountains crumble into the sea.*
> *Let the oceans roar and foam.*
> > *Let the mountains tremble as the waters surge! . . .*
> *The nations are in chaos,*
> > *and their kingdoms crumble!*
> *God's voice thunders,*
> > *and the earth melts!*
> *The LORD of Heaven's Armies is here among us;*
> > *the God of Israel is our fortress."*

We praise your holy name that we have nothing to fear. Amen.

DISCUSSION GUIDE

WEEK 1: PREPARE TO BE SENT & DO A REALITY CHECK
Prepare to Be Sent

1. As you look at the state of our world today, what are you most afraid of? Is there something you fear that seems closer to home or is present in your everyday life?

2. Chaplain Black points us to the verse where Jesus encourages us to "keep watch and pray, so that you will not give into temptation." Is there an area of your life where you can begin the practice of warding off evil? How can your surrounding community support you?

3. Chaplain Black says, "Regardless of life's challenges, we can remain fearless by taking our problems to Jesus." What are some of the obstacles holding you back from taking your problems to Jesus? How can we support each other and hold each other accountable in this practice?

4. Do you ever feel a nudge or prompting from God? What's your usual reaction—negligence, reluctance, or prompt obedience? How is your reaction keeping you in a place of fear?

5. Where has God surprised you lately? How has it affected your relationship with him?

6. In what ways do you feel like a lamb among wolves in the cultural climate today?

7. Chaplain Black points to the parable Jesus tells of the scattered seeds. Which type of soil resonates with you most as you consider your own faith journey? Explain.

8. How can you be a light bearer in this dark and threatening world? Are there small practical ways in which you can begin shining that light in your own community today?

9. In Chapter 3, Chaplain Black encourages us to adopt a fearless principle of spending or investing our lives, not hoarding them. As you look at the way you live your life, do you spend your life or hoard it? When you consider your gifts, how can they be used to contribute to the world around you?

Do a Reality Check

1. What does the word *love* mean to you? Talk with your group about the greatest example of love in your life.

2. It can be hard to demonstrate real love and show your true identity, especially in today's society. Amid racial tension, terrorist attacks, and a general fear of the future, what are some tangible ways we can love people the way God calls us to?

3. What does it mean to fear the Lord? How is that different from the fear we feel about our circumstances?

4. Chaplain Black notes that a principle of living fearlessly is making family a priority. Whether it's the family you were born into or the family you've created for yourself, what can you do daily to live out this principle?

5. When we experience loss and sorrow in our lives, we must choose between *rescue* and *ruin* as we look toward our future. When have you chosen to be rescued by God?

WEEK 2: THRIVE IN A PREDATORY WORLD & BE AS WISE AS A SERPENT

Thrive in a Predatory World

1. Part of living fearlessly, Chaplain Black suggests, is having a purposeful prayer life. It should include a combination of adoration, confession, supplication, and submission. As you read through Chaplain Black's description of each practice, which do you find yourself struggling with most? Why do you think that

is? Talk with your group about how you can support one another in strengthening these areas.

2. In Chapter 8, Chaplain Black says that to "break the devil's grip, expect Jesus to push you out of your comfort zone." How is God calling you out of your comfort zone in your places of fear?

3. Has God seemed to say no to your prayers? How did that experience affect your relationship with him? How do we trust God when our prayers seem to go unanswered, especially if they're prayers against feelings of fear?

4. As you look back on your life so far, what is the testimony of deliverance you can bless others with?

5. Which of your past experiences do you consider to be "one of life's tests"? How did it prepare you for greater service to those in your community?

6. Chaplain Black suggests that self-denial is a part of living fearlessly. In what ways can you practice—and support others— in this difficult calling? How can self-denial help you in your walk toward a fearless life?

Be as Wise as a Serpent

1. Do you believe that God will protect you? Where can you see that God has protected you in the past, even if you were unaware?

2. When we feel afraid or threatened, we can cling to the many promises that God has written in the Bible. Which specific promise has been most helpful to you in times of fear or despair?

3. In times of distress, it's easy to let our minds wander anxiously to the worst-case scenario. Think of the most recent time this has happened to you. Did your fears come to fruition? How can we encourage one another in these times and "share each other's burdens"?

4. How is God sanctifying you in this season? How could you use specific prayer?

5. In Chapter 13, Chaplain Black urges us to give sacrificially and recklessly, like the widow in Mark 12 or Mary's gift of ointment

in John 12. Even though it can be scary and make you feel vulnerable, what is one way you can give recklessly over the next week?

WEEK 3: BE AS INNOCENT AS A DOVE

1. Chaplain Black presents pride as one of the many reasons we may fail to thrive in a threatening world. Where do you see symptoms of this sneaky sin in your own actions? How can we support each other in pursuing humility?

2. In Chapter 15, Chaplain Black suggests that the fall to sin, especially the sin of lust, "may seem to happen suddenly and overnight, but pernicious gradations exist that lead to ruin." Exploring the fall of David, he outlines the anatomy of a fall. Which of these missteps do you struggle most with in your own life? If you feel comfortable, share with your group.

3. In this age of online streaming and social media, it's easy to allow the sin of sloth to creep into our daily lives. Yet the consequences of this seemingly inconsequential tendency can be enormously detrimental. In what ways have you seen laziness negatively affect your life? Which of the "fearless principles" could use strengthening in your life—and how will you go about making the change?

4. When we look at the state of our world—or even our own lives— we can fall prey to destructive anger. Chaplain Black encourages us to develop compassion even in the midst of our anger. How can we realistically "permit anger to disturb our spirit into compassionate action"? Brainstorm practical acts of compassion with your group, and commit to carrying out at least one throughout the week.

5. What (or who) makes you most envious? How does comparison affect your daily life?

WEEK 4: CONCENTRATE ON THE TASK & PERSEVERE THROUGH REJECTION

Concentrate on the Task

1. If we want to change the world, we must learn to be comfortable

evangelizing for our faith. What are some of the fears holding you back from witnessing to your friends, family, or neighbors?

2. What do you consider to be your sphere of influence? How can you intentionally work at widening that circle?

3. Chaplain Black writes, "What comes out of your mouths is instructive." In what ways are your words red flags for your spiritual life? How can we hold one another accountable for what we say?

4. Race relations is an ever-present source of tension and fear in our country—and in recent years, it has only become more of a prevalent issue. How can we imitate Christ and strengthen cross-cultural relationships?

5. Forgiveness is one of the most difficult commands Jesus calls us to. Why are we so reluctant to forgive those who have wronged us? Whom do you need to forgive today?

Persevere through Rejection

1. How do you deal with broken dreams? How does that contribute to your fear of this threatening world?

2. Chaplain Black says that if we want to "stay fearless in a dangerous environment," we must consciously shift our focus back to Jesus. What are some practical steps we can take toward this shift in perspective?

3. When have you been given a gracious second chance? How have you, in turn, given others second chances?

4. As you worked through Chaplain Black's reflections, what was most helpful in teaching you how to live in this threatening world? How do you view your fears and questions about the future differently?

NOTES

AUTHOR'S NOTE

1. Winston Churchill, speech to the House of Commons, May 13, 1940; www .winstonchurchill.org/resources/speeches /233-1940-the-finest-hou/92-blood-toil -tears-and-sweat.
2. Matthew 10:16, ESV.
3. John 16:33
4. Ibid.
5. 2 Timothy 3:12
6. Psalm 119:105
7. Romans 5:3-4
8. John 10:11-15; 1 Samuel 17:32-37
9. Psalm 23:4
10. Luke 9:1-6

CHAPTER 1: *Prepare for Some Paradoxes*

1. Matthew 10:16, ESV.
2. Ephesians 2:8-9
3. 1 Peter 1:18-19
4. Romans 8:32, NIV.
5. Psalm 84:11, NIV.
6. John 16:12
7. Romans 10:2, ESV.
8. Matthew 26:41
9. 1 Peter 5:8-9
10. James 4:7-10
11. Ephesians 3:20

CHAPTER 2: *Prepare for Some Surprises*

1. "I Believe," written by Ervin Drake, Al Stillman, Irvin Graham, and Jimmy Shirl, © copyright 1953 by Hampshire House Publishing Corp. All rights reserved. Used by permission of TRO, Inc.
2. Ephesians 3:20, NIV, ESV.
3. Psalm 84:11
4. James 4:13-15, NIV.
5. Matthew 17:20
6. Philippians 4:19
7. Jeremiah 29:11; Ephesians 3:20
8. Psalm 23:1
9. Malachi 3:10
10. 1 Corinthians 10:13
11. 1 Corinthians 2:14
12. Genesis 22:13
13. John 14:1-3; 1 Thessalonians 5:2
14. Matthew 24:27, NIV.
15. John 2:1-2, NIV.
16. Nehemiah 8:10
17. 2 Samuel 6:14
18. John 10:10, NIV.
19. John 4:13-14, NIV.
20. John 5:6, NIV.
21. John 5:8
22. We can infer the completeness of the man's healing by his presence at the Temple (spiritual) and his interaction with the Jewish leaders (spiritual and social), who had not paid him any mind during his almost four decades lying beside the pool, but who now engaged him in conversation—even if it was an interrogation.
23. John 2:3; 1 Peter 5:7.
24. Psalm 50:15
25. James 4:2, NIV.
26. John 2:4
27. John 2:5

28. John 2:6-7
29. Luke 5:4
30. Luke 5:5
31. Luke 5:6
32. John 2:10
33. 1 Corinthians 10:31
34. Numbers 20:1-12
35. Matthew 17:1-9
36. Psalm 84:11, NIV.

CHAPTER 3: *Prepare the Soil of Your Heart*
1. Genesis 1:28
2. Matthew 7:20
3. John 15:5
4. 1 Corinthians 3:6
5. Psalm 27:14
6. 2 Peter 1:5-8, CEV.
7. Genesis 1:28
8. Acts 13:36
9. Ephesians 3:20
10. Matthew 13:5-6, author's paraphrase.
11. Romans 14:5
12. Luke 14:28, CEV.
13. Luke 10:27
14. Isaiah 1:18, ESV.
15. Luke 10:41-42, CEV.
16. Matthew 13:8
17. Matthew 13:23
18. James 1:22-24, CEV.
19. Matthew 5:13-16, CEV.
20. Genesis 19:1-29
21. Matthew 5:13-16
22. Isaiah 58:7-10
23. 1 Peter 4:10-11
24. Matthew 16:24-25
25. Matthew 16:24, ESV, NIV.
26. Matthew 26:72, CEV.
27. Romans 6:11, CEV. Italics added.
28. Acts 20:35
29. Matthew 5:47
30. Matthew 5:41, NIV.
31. Matthew 5:44-46
32. Kahlil Gibran, *The Prophet* (New York: Alfred A. Knopf, 1923), 19.

CHAPTER 4: *Embrace Love*
1. 1 Corinthians 13:7-8, NIV.
2. Matthew 25:37-39

3. Romans 12:1, ESV.
4. 2 Corinthians 9:7
5. 1 Corinthians 13:4-5
6. John 14:15
7. John 13:35
8. John Oxenham, "In Christ There Is No East or West" (1908).
9. Sabine Baring-Gould, "Onward, Christian Soldiers" (1865), stanza 3, line 3.
10. Revelation 7:9-10
11. 1 Corinthians 7:7; 3:13
12. 1 Corinthians 12:31–13:1, NIV.
13. John 13:34, NIV.
14. Matthew 5:44, NKJV.
15. Matthew 22:37, NIV; Matthew 22:39, NIV.
16. Romans 13:10; Galatians 5:14

CHAPTER 5: *Prepare to Serve*
1. Acts 13:22
2. John 4:23
3. Job 1:8
4. Genesis 24:1-67
5. Luke 1:5-21
6. Luke 1:26-38
7. Proverbs 1:7, author's paraphrase.
8. Hebrews 12:1
9. Job 1:8
10. Job 1:8
11. 1 Corinthians 4:1, ESV.
12. Colossians 3:23-24, CEV.
13. Job 1:21, CEV.
14. Job 2:9-10.
15. Mark 5:19, CEV.
16. Genesis 33:13-14, CEV.
17. Alfred Tennyson, "Morte d'Arthur," lines 247-248, in *Poems, 4th edition* (London: Moxon, 1845).
18. James 5:17
19. 1 Kings 18:41-44
20. Matthew 25:14-30
21. 2 Peter 1:5-7, CEV.
22. Matthew 25:8, CEV.
23. Matthew 25:9, CEV.

CHAPTER 6: *Choose Rescue over Ruin*
1. Psalm 51:5, NKJV.
2. 1 Corinthians 15:22, NKJV.
3. Ibid.

4. Romans 5:19, NIV.
5. Romans 7:18-19
6. Romans 6:23
7. Proverbs 8:13
8. NIV
9. Luke 23:39-43
10. John 15:16
11. John 6:44
12. Philippians 2:13
13. John 3:16-17
14. James Rowe, "Love Lifted Me" (1912). Public domain.
15. Romans 5:20

CHAPTER 7: *Punctuate Your Life with Purposeful Prayer*

1. 1 Thessalonians 5:16, KJV.
2. 1 Thessalonians 5:19, KJV.
3. 1 Thessalonians 5:20, KJV.
4. 1 Thessalonians 5:22, KJV.
5. Ralph Waldo Emerson, "Pray Without Ceasing," in *Ralph Waldo Emerson: Selected Essays, Lectures, and Poems* (New York: Bantam Books, 1990), 61.
6. Psalm 34:1, ESV.
7. Isaiah 26:3, ESV.
8. 1 John 1:9
9. Isaiah 59:2
10. Nehemiah 1:6-7
11. Ezra 9:6
12. Nehemiah 1:11
13. Isaiah 45:9
14. Psalm 40:8
15. Proverbs 3:5-6
16. Psalm 5:12
17. Matthew 26:38
18. Matthew 26:39
19. Ibid.
20. Luke 23:46, NIV.
21. Psalm 84:11, NIV.

CHAPTER 8: *Break the Devil's Grip*

1. Matthew 13:28
2. 1 Peter 5:8.
3. Luke 10:18
4. Mark 5:2
5. Mark 5:9
6. Hosea 4:6, ESV.

7. 2 Corinthians 2:11, NIV.
8. Isaiah 14:13
9. Revelation 12:12
10. Hebrews 7:25
11. Luke 22:31-32
12. Psalm 51:5
13. Romans 7:18-19
14. Luke 18:18, NIV.
15. Luke 18:22, NIV.
16. John 4:16-18
17. Luke 2:35
18. 2 Timothy 3:12
19. Matthew 10:36
20. James 2:19
21. Luke 10:17
22. Luke 10:18, 20
23. Mark 5:19
24. Job 13:15, CEV.
25. Martin Luther, "A Mighty Fortress Is Our God," (1529), stanza 3. Public domain.
26. 2 Corinthians 1:3-4, NIV.
27. John 4:29
28. John 4:30
29. Martin Luther, "A Mighty Fortress Is Our God," (1529), stanza 3, composite translation from the *Pennsylvania Lutheran Church Book* (1868). Public domain.

CHAPTER 9: *Pass Life's Tests*

1. Genesis 22
2. Esther 4
3. 1 Samuel 17
4. 2 Timothy 3:12
5. John 16:33
6. Proverbs 13:15, NKJV.
7. Luke 22:33
8. Luke 22:34
9. Luke 22:32; Acts 2:14-41
10. Mark 14:29
11. Job 14:1
12. 1 Peter 4:12
13. Matthew 16:21
14. Matthew 4
15. Matthew 4:1
16. Matthew 4:11
17. Luke 2:51
18. Luke 2:52

19. Genesis 24:19-20
20. Daniel 6:10
21. Matthew 16:24
22. Daniel 1:7, 3:1-30, 6:1-28

CHAPTER 10: *Succeed in Slippery Places*
1. See Genesis 39 and 2 Samuel 11.
2. See Acts 5 and Genesis 13.
3. See Judges 14:5-6 and 1 Samuel 17:32-36.
4. Isaiah 54:17, NIV.
5. Romans 8:38-39, NKJV.
6. Frederick M. Lehman, "The Love of God" (1917). Public domain.
7. Psalm 73:24, NIV.
8. Isaiah 30:21, CEV.
9. Matthew 2:8
10. Psalm 73:16-17, NKJV.
11. Isaiah 6:8, ESV.
12. Ibid.
13. Mark 8:36
14. Daniel 4:30, ESV.
15. Psalm 73:27-28, NIV.
16. Matthew 14:30.
17. Hebrews 13:5, ESV.
18. Matthew 28:20, NKJV.
19. See Psalm 23.
20. Psalm 16:11, ESV.
21. Isaiah 26:3
22. Leila Naylor Morris, "Nearer, Still Nearer" (1898). Public domain.

CHAPTER 11: *Find Deliverance from Distress*
1. John 16:33, NIV.
2. See 2 Corinthians 1:3-4.
3. John 13:35
4. Psalm 4:1
5. Psalm 50:15
6. Psalm 4:2, NIV.
7. 2 Timothy 1:7-8
8. Nehemiah 6:2-3, ESV.
9. 1 Samuel 17:45-47
10. 1 Peter 2:9, NIV.
11. Psalm 4:4, CEV.
12. KJV
13. Genesis 39:9
14. Psalm 4:7-8

15. Job 23:10
16. Psalm 4:8
17. Proverbs 27:1
18. Matthew 6:34
19. Psalm 31:15

CHAPTER 12: *Conquer Fear*
1. Minnie Louise Haskins, "God Knows" (1908).
2. Matthew 2:2, ESV.
3. Mark 9:39
4. John 10:16
5. Job 23:10, ESV.
6. Luke 23:46
7. Ephesians 2:10, ESV.
8. Proverbs 3:5-8, ESV.
9. 1 Kings 17:9, ESV.
10. See 1 Kings 16:31 and Luke 4:25-26.
11. ESV
12. Luke 5:4, ESV.
13. Luke 5:5, ESV.
14. Job 14:1, CEV.
15. 2 Timothy 3:12, ESV.
16. William Shakespeare, *Hamlet*, act III, scene 1, lines 1750-1751. Public domain.
17. James 4:13
18. See 1 Thessalonians 4:13-14.

CHAPTER 13: *Give More with Less*
1. Mark 12:41-44, NIV.
2. 1 Corinthians 13:3
3. 1 Kings 17:9, ESV.
4. Luke 4:25-26, ESV.
5. 2 Corinthians 9:7, ESV.
6. 1 Timothy 6:7
7. Mark 12:44
8. Luke 10:25-37
9. Matthew 16:24, ESV.
10. Dietrich Bonhoeffer, *The Cost of Discipleship* (New York: Touchstone, 1995), 89.
11. Luke 18:18-23
12. Luke 18:22, ESV.
13. John 12:1-8
14. John 12:5, author's paraphrase.
15. John 12:7-8, CEV.
16. Ecclesiastes 11:1, ESV.
17. Ibid., NIV.

18. James Allan Francis, *One Solitary Life* (Chicago: Le Petit Oiseau Press, 1963), 7.
19. Philippians 2:6-8

CHAPTER 14: *Live without Pride*

1. Howard Breck, "Rasheed Wallace Guarantees Victory, Again," *New York Times*, May 15, 2006; http://www.nytimes.com/2006/05/15/sports/basketball/15nba.html.
2. Tom Withers, Associated Press, "Wallace can't live up to guarantee as Cavaliers even series," *USA Today*, May 16, 2006; http://usatoday30.usatoday.com/sports/basketball/playoffs/2006-05-15-pistons-cavaliers-game4_x.htm.
3. 1 Corinthians 10:12, ESV.
4. Genesis 3:6
5. Genesis 27:1-40
6. Acts 12:21-23
7. Acts 12:22
8. Acts 12:23
9. Blaise Pascal, "Thoughts," 347.
10. Howard E. Butt, "The Art of Being A Big Shot," speech at the Layman's Institute, Dallas, 1963. Quoted in David Jeremiah, *What to Do When You Don't Know What to Do* (Colorado Springs: David C. Cook, 2016), 224.
11. 1 John 2:16
12. Obadiah 1:3
13. 1 Samuel 17:41-51
14. Isaiah 36-37
15. Proverbs 13:10
16. Mark 6:1-6
17. 2 Samuel 11:1–12:12
18. Genesis 39:10
19. Judges 16
20. Matthew 6:13, ESV, NIV.
21. 2 Corinthians 10:12, NKJV.
22. John 15:5
23. Acts 9:6, NKJV.
24. Matthew 26:75
25. Proverbs 13:10, CEV.

CHAPTER 15: *Live without Lust*

1. Numbers 12:1-16
2. 1 Samuel 13:14
3. 2 Samuel 6:11-15
4. 1 Samuel 24:4-6
5. 1 Corinthians 10:13
6. 1 Kings 19:18, NKJV.
7. 2 Samuel 11:1, NIV.
8. 1 Peter 2:9
9. 2 Samuel 11:11
10. 2 Samuel 11:2, CEV.
11. Romans 14:23
12. 2 Samuel 11:10-13
13. 2 Samuel 11:14-27
14. 2 Samuel 12:1-12
15. 1 John 1:9

CHAPTER 16: *Live without Sloth*

1. Frank Lewis Dyer and Thomas Commerford Martin, *Edison: His Life and Inventions*, vol. 2 (New York: Harper & Bros., 1910), 607.
2. Kahlil Gibran, *The Prophet* (New York: Alfred A. Knopf, 1923), 25.
3. Proverbs 14:23, NIV.
4. Proverbs 18:9, NKJV.
5. Proverbs 26:16, NKJV.
6. NKJV
7. Proverbs 14:23, NKJV.
8. NKJV
9. Proverbs 24:30-34
10. Luke 22

CHAPTER 17: *Live without Destructive Anger*

1. Mark 3:5
2. Genesis 37
3. Exodus 5:6-9
4. Daniel 3:19-23
5. Jonah 4:1-4, CEV.
6. Jonah 3:4
7. Jonah 4:6-11, CEV.
8. Matthew 25:31-46
9. Ephesians 4:26-27, CEV.
10. 1 Samuel 20:33
11. Mark 11:15-19
12. Ephesians 4:26
13. Psalm 30:5

CHAPTER 18: *Live without Greed*

1. CEV
2. Luke 12:15, ESV.

3. ESV

4. 1 Timothy 6:8, ESV.

5. 2 Kings 5:20, 22, author's paraphrase.

6. 2 Kings 5:25-27, author's paraphrase.

7. Romans 6:1-2, NIV.

8. See Leviticus 10:1; Numbers 26:60-61; 1 Samuel 2:12-15.

9. Exodus 20:17

10. NKJV

11. Romans 12:15, NKJV.

12. Galatians 6:7

13. ESV

CHAPTER 19: *Live without Gluttony*

1. 1 Peter 4:3

2. Ecclesiastes 4:6, NIV.

3. Genesis 25:34

4. 1 Corinthians 10:31

5. Matthew 4:4

6. 2 Corinthians 4:18

7. 1 Corinthians 9:25, 27, ESV.

8. Galatians 5:22-23

9. Philippians 4:19

CHAPTER 20: *Live without Envy*

1. Genesis 4:2-7

2. Genesis 30:1

3. Genesis 29:30; 30:15, 20

4. Numbers 12:1-2; Daniel 6:1-5

5. Matthew 22:15; 26:3-4; 27:1, 17-18

6. Genesis 37:1-11

7. Genesis 41

8. Matthew 10:36, ESV.

9. 1 Samuel 17:28, CEV.

10. John 11:47-53

11. Genesis 39

12. Proverbs 6:6, NIV.

13. Psalm 5:12, NIV.

14. Psalm 34:5, 7-9, 15, 17

15. Jonathan Edwards, "Resolutions" (1716), in *Letters and Personal Writings*, WJE Online, vol. 16, ed., George S. Claghorn; http://edwards.yale.edu/rchive?path =aHR0cDovL2Vkd2FyZHMueWFsZS 5lZHUvY2dpLWJpbi9uZXdaaGlsby 9nZXRvbmplY3QuGw/Yy4xNTo3 NDoxLndqZW8=.

16. Psalm 19:13

17. Genesis 49:29–50:21

18. Genesis 50:20

CHAPTER 21: *Live a Less Complicated Life*

1. Job 14:1

2. John 16:33

3. "Hans Hofmann: Quotes," www.hanshof mann.net/quotes.html#.V4y5APkrK9I.

4. John Keble, "New Every Morning Is the Love" (1822). Public domain.

5. Henry David Thoreau, *Walden* (1854), Simon & Brown reprint edition (Hollywood, FL: Simon & Brown, 2011), 61.

6. Gilbert Robinson, conversation with the author, date unknown.

7. Ephesians 5:16.

8. Freddie C. Colston, *Dr. Benjamin E. Mays Speaks: Representative Speeches of a Great American Orator* (Lanham, MD: University Press of America, 2002), 150.

9. 1 Timothy 6:8

10. Ecclesiastes 4:6, NIV.

11. John 3:16-17

12. John 14:2-3, ESV.

13. 1 John 3:1-2

14. Acts 1:8

15. Matthew 6:21

16. 2 Peter 1:4

17. Malachi 3:10

18. Blaise Pascal, *Les Pensées de Blaise Pascal*, Fragment Divertissement No. 4/7; www .penseesdepascal.fr/Divertissement/ Divertissement4-moderne.php. Translated from the French by Google Translate.

19. Luke 22:39-46

20. Exodus 16:11-21

21. Psalm 90:12, NIV.

22. Matthew 24:44

23. "How I Want World to Remember Me: Speech by Dr. King," *Chicago Tribune*, April 7, 1968, sec. 1, p. 9.

24. Matthew 6:25, ESV.

25. Exodus 18:22-23

26. Acts 6:2-3, NIV.

27. Luke 7:36-50

28. Proverbs 10:9, NIV.

29. Psalm 5:12, author's paraphrase.

30. 1 Samuel 2:30; Galatians 6:7
31. 2 Timothy 4:6-8, NIV.

CHAPTER 22: *Strive to Belong to God's Family*
1. Matthew 12:47-50
2. 1 John 3:2, NIV.
3. 2 Samuel 9:1
4. 2 Samuel 9:3-5
5. 2 Samuel 9:7, NIV.
6. Psalm 51:5
7. John 3:17
8. John 20:21, NIV.
9. John 13:35
10. 1 Corinthians 12:7, compare NIV, ESV, and NLT.
11. 1 Corinthians 12:4-6, 18-20
12. John 17:21-23, NIV.
13. Hebrews 3:13, NIV.
14. ESV
15. James 5:19-20
16. CEV
17. Matthew 10:1, 7-8
18. 2 Corinthians 8:5, NIV.
19. Luke 10:42, NIV.

CHAPTER 23: *Change Your World*
1. Acts 13:36, NIV.
2. Martin Luther King Jr., speech at Cobo Hall, Detroit, MI, June 23, 1963; http://kingencyclopedia.stanford.edu /encyclopedia/documentsentry/doc_ speech_at_the_great_march_on_detroit/.
3. Matthew 5:13-14
4. Acts 1:4-5
5. 2 Corinthians 5:17
6. John 15:16
7. John 6:44
8. Philippians 2:13
9. Acts 1:8
10. Acts 19:6
11. Luke 11:13
12. See Dawn Ortiz, "Beggars Telling Other Beggars Where to Find Bread?" *RealRealityZone*, December 26, 2010; www.realrealityzone.com/2010/12 /beggars-telling-other-beggars-where-to -find-bread/.

13. Acts 1:8
14. John 12:32
15. Galatians 6:14
16. Rev. James C. Perkins, "Personal Reflections on the Life and Ministry of Dr. Gardner C. Taylor," in *Gardner C. Taylor: Submissions to the Dean*, eds., J. Douglas Wiley and Ivan Douglas Hicks (Chicago: UMI, 2009), 189.
17. 1 Corinthians 2:2, NIV.
18. Mark 6:4, ESV.
19. Mark 6:3, CEV.
20. Mark 6:2, CEV.
21. Mark 6:5
22. Matthew 28:19
23. 2 Corinthians 5:19-20
24. John 20:21

CHAPTER 24: *Start a Conspiracy of Kindness*
1. Genesis 4:8; 27:41
2. Genesis 37:18-28
3. 2 Samuel 13:1-39
4. Estimates vary for all these wars. Sources here include the Civil War Trust; necrometrics.com; National WWII Museum; http://www.nationalww2 museum.org/learn/education/for-students /ww2-history/ww2-by-the-numbers/world -wide-deaths.html?referrer=https://www .google.com/.
5. Estimates vary for all these wars. Sources here include Human Rights Watch; the *New York Times*; and *National Geographic*.
6. Romans 7:18
7. Ephesians 6:12
8. Matthew 16:23
9. Romans 12:21
10. Proverbs 16:32, ESV.
11. Jonah 3:10–4:11
12. Jonah 4:9, 11
13. Genesis 37:1-11
14. 1 Peter 5:8
15. Luke 22:31; 54-62; Ephesians 6:11
16. Ephesians 4:29, NIV.
17. ESV

18. Sigmund Freud, *A General Introduction to Psychoanalysis*, trans. G. Stanley Hall (New York: Boni and Liveright, 1920), 3.

19. 1 Samuel 23:17

20. Matthew 12:36

21. Martin Luther King Jr. interview on *Meet the Press*, April 17, 1960; transcribed on July 21, 2016, from www.youtube.com/watch?v=1q881g1L_d8.

22. Galatians 3:28

23. John 4:7-9, NIV.

24. Matthew 6:12, ESV.

25. Matthew 18:28

26. See Genesis 27:41; 31:36-42; 32:1-8

27. Luke 15:30

28. Mathew 18:21

29. Acts 7:60, NIV.

30. Luke 6:27-28, NIV.

CHAPTER 25: *Deal with Broken Dreams*

1. Proverbs 29:18, KJV.

2. This familiar sounding line, often attributed to Robert F. Kennedy, who used a version in some of his campaign speeches, is adapted from George Bernard Shaw, *Back to Methuselah: A Metabiological Pentateuch*, vol. 2 (New York: Brentano's, 1922), 6.

3. Luke 19:29-30, NIV.

4. Luke 14:28

5. Matthew 26:14-16, 21, 34

6. Luke 19:38, ESV.

7. Matthew 14:28

8. 1 Samuel 17:1-50

9. Matthew 4:4

10. Psalm 119:105

11. Matthew 6:10, ESV.

12. John 5:30

13. Luke 23:46, NIV.

14. Job 23:10, NIV.

15. Jeremiah 1:4-5

16. Luke 22:42

17. Daniel 3:17-18

18. Luke 19:39, author's paraphrase.

19. Luke 19:40, author's paraphrase.

20. See Galatians 6:9

CHAPTER 26: *Seize Life's Second Chances*

1. 2 Samuel 24:14

2. John 8:7

3. Ezekiel 33:11

4. Psalm 103:17, KJV.

5. John 8:4-5

6. John 12:5

7. John 12:6

8. Matthew 5:7

9. Jonah 4:1-3

10. Jonah 4:10-11, author's paraphrase.

11. John 8:7

12. John 8:11, NIV.

13. Mark 3:5, NIV.

14. Romans 2:4

15. 2 Corinthians 5:14, NIV.

16. Matthew 6:12, ESV.

17. Matthew 18:21

18. Matthew 18:22

19. Luke 10:17

20. Luke 10:18-20

21. Philippians 2:13, ESV.

ABOUT THE AUTHOR

Barry C. Black has served as chaplain of the United States Senate since 2003. Prior to coming to Capitol Hill, Chaplain Black served in the US Navy for more than twenty-seven years, ending his distinguished career as the chief of Navy chaplains. While in the Navy, he ministered to members of the military and their families throughout the United States, Europe, and Asia. His military decorations include the Navy Distinguished Service Medal, the Legion of Merit Medal, and two Defense Meritorious Service Medals. In addition to master of arts degrees in divinity, counseling, and management, he has earned doctorates in ministry and psychology. Chaplain Black has been recognized for many outstanding achievements, including the 1995 NAACP Renowned Service Award for his contribution to equal opportunity and civil rights. He also received the 2002 Benjamin Elijah Mays Distinguished Leadership Award from the Morehouse School of Religion. He is the author of *From the Hood to the Hill* and *The Blessing of Adversity.* Chaplain Black and his wife have three sons.